ALL

IN

"Pat Gohn knocks it out of the park with this honest and compelling treatment of our disappointments with the Church. She offers encouragement for staying Catholic and engaging in an active faith life for our sake and the sake of Christ's Bride, the Church."

Kelly Wahlquist
Founder of WINE: Women In the New Evangelization and editor of *Walk in Her Sandals*

"We humans acknowledge that we are 'body, mind, and spirit' and, as such, when we're nourishing our bodies, we seek out what is 'all natural.' When we pursue wisdom, philosophy, and healing, we look for what is 'whole' and 'wholistic.' When we tend to our spirit, we search for what is 'sacred' and 'holy.' With *All In*, Pat Gohn has managed, through simple personal stories and the application of her fine reasoning skills, to prove that the Catholic Church perfectly answers the modern quest for the natural, the whole, and the holy. *All In* is a book full of warmth and clarity that, to a mind that is open, can be a true revelation and a great assist in the journey toward the fullness of Truth."

Elizabeth Scalia
Editor-in-chief of *Aleteia* and author of *Strange Gods*

"More than a spiritual guidebook, *All In* tells a great love story—and the lovers at the heart of it are God and his people. With clarity, wisdom, candor, and joy, Pat Gohn reminds us that to fall in love with the Lord is to be 'all in' love. Count me as someone who was won over by this wise book's tender charms and penetrating good sense. I'm all in for *All In*, and I think a lot of people will be, too!"

Deacon Greg Kandra
Catholic blogger and journalist at *Aleteia*

"Pat Gohn quotes scripture and cites the *Catechism* in the intimate way a good friend shares happy news over a cup of coffee. When she shares why staying in the Church and actively participating in the faith is essential for all of us, I am—as her title suggests—all in."

Maria Morera Johnson
Author of *My Badass Book of Saints*

PAT GOHN

Author of *Blessed, Beautiful, and Bodacious*

ALL

> WHY BELONGING TO THE CATHOLIC CHURCH MATTERS

IN

AVE MARIA PRESS AVE Notre Dame, Indiana

Scripture quotations are from *New Revised Standard Version Bible, Catholic Edition* copyright © 1989 National Council of the Churches of Christ in the United States of America. Used by permission. All rights reserved.

Founded in 1865, Ave Maria Press is a ministry of the United States Province of Holy Cross.

www.avemariapress.com

Paperback: ISBN-13 978-1-59471-677-5

E-book: ISBN-13 978-1-59471-678-2

Cover image © Shutterstock.

Interior by Katherine Robinson.

Cover by Katherine Ross.

Printed and bound in the United States of America.

Library of Congress Cataloging-in-Publication Data is available.

For my family

The Church truly knows that only God,
Whom she serves,
meets the deepest longings of the human heart,
which is never fully satisfied
by what this world has to offer.

Gaudium et Spes, 41

CONTENTS

WHAT'S DRIVING
THIS BOOK?

For Bob and me, a fair amount of our courtship was spent with me looking at my honey's rear end as he bent over the hood of his car, tinkering. I'm not trying to be rude or lewd here. I'm just stating a fact. To this day, my husband, Bob, is enamored with MGs. Beyond that he enjoys all things related to little British sports cars. They have captured his imagination since he owned his first MGB in college. Sure, it was a fun date car back then. But it broke down fairly frequently. Bob did all the maintenance and repairs himself; so often, when I was waiting on Bob, it was because Bob was waiting on the MG.

We married sometime after he owned that first "B"—a car that he loved but sold to save money. Back then we were trying to be responsible adults. Keeping an older car running, one that was no longer made, was just getting too much for the budget. You know that selling it was for love, right? That he gave up that car for the sake of *us*? But I digress.

It wasn't long after we got our finances in order that I realized Bob's first MG had left him smitten. Like it or not, I was married to a car guy. Not just any cars, mind you— vintage British cars. He still talks about the one that got away, that first 1970 MGB-GT, British racing green, hardtop.

1

Fast forward to today. Our marriage has expanded and grown to welcome children, in-laws, friends, and pets. It even stretched to include five successive MGBs—four were ragtops. A few were clunkers that Bob, quite literally, raised from the dead. We did not have a lot of spare cash to throw into this hobby, so Bob had to be resourceful. He read manuals, fixed things, and retooled old parts or purchased used parts.

That includes the little white '77 MGB we own now. He bought it from a fellow who wanted to dump it after a fire in the engine. Bob, the consummate optimist, found a way to rebuild it for very little money and the proverbial elbow grease, forever etching in my mind that one man's trash is another man's treasure.

For Bob, having an MG is not just about car owner-ship. It's about restoring it, making it new again. It's—dare I say it?—a *relationship*.

Over the years I have watched, with fascination, Bob's dedication to a car, often through long periods of it not run-ning *at all*. I've been inspired by his long-suffering through seasons where engine or body parts were strewn all over the floor of our garage in various phases of restoration and, er, desperation.

I have been on call for many test-drives after a motor repair—just to be sure that he gets back home and does not need a rescue from the side of the road somewhere. And yes, I have often helped push-start the thing out of the driveway, and once, out of a ditch on the side of a hill. (If the truth be told about that time, I was behind the wheel. I accidently backed it downhill and into said ditch. Those MG clutches can be so temperamental.)

Slowly, over time, I have grown to love this hobby of my husband's, mostly because I love Bob.

I want to love the things that Bob loves. I've taken time to get to know his interests from the inside out as best as I can. I have handed him greasy tools when he's been under the car. I have attended car shows. I can name several British car models just by looking at them. I can hear from the purr of the engine when it is running smoothly or when it has a subtle miss or mild roughness. I know how to order parts from the Moss catalog and eBay. I have even ordered specialty items to delight this man at Christmas. Once, in a moment of crazy indulgence, I dropped $350, plus shipping, on a custom classic wood-grained steering wheel. I did it because I knew it was something he would never do for his thrifty self.

So, it seems, I have caught the fever. I've changed. I love what my love loves.

In the final analysis, I receive the ultimate recompense, and I truly benefit from this love of all things MG. I have a husband who wants to go out on dates to distant destinations that I propose just so he can have the pleasure of taking me there. For years, we've both looked forward to top-down drives on sunny afternoons, zipping down twisty country lanes, exploring New England. My guy loves it when I ride shotgun.

So what does this all have to do with being all in as a Catholic?

Let it remind you of how we can change over time. Let it illustrate how we can slowly come to love someone or something over time—and how our own love or friendship for someone can hold sway in shaping our opinions about something we might not otherwise come to on our own.

Faith is a lot like love. Faith is more often *caught* than taught.

The first followers of Jesus Christ were initially caught by the attraction of Jesus' message and witness. Those first apostles were the earliest members of the Church. They were so confident in their beliefs that eleven of Jesus' twelve apostles died as martyrs for the faith.

That's all in.

All in is confident certainty. It is assurance and trust. When it comes to being a Catholic Christian—a follower of Jesus—belonging to the Catholic Church is the confident anchor that holds one steady. The Church is a stronghold of reliable truth and is sure footing on solid ground in a troubled world.

THE ONE THING

In the 1991 movie *City Slickers*, Billy Crystal plays Mitch, a married urbanite searching for the meaning of his belea-guered life. He and his friends escape the routines of city life by signing on as ranch hands on a cattle drive. The real cowboy in the film, Curly, gives Mitch some advice while out on the trail, and it becomes the dominant theme for the movie.

> Curly: Do you know what the secret of life is? [*Holds up one finger.*] This.
> Mitch: Your finger?
> Curly: One thing. Just one thing. You stick to that and the rest don't mean [diddly].
> Mitch: But, what is the "one thing"?
> Curly: [*smiles*] That's what you have to find out.

It's a great scene, and it fosters all kinds of great questions.

What's your one thing? What's the secret of life? What brings you the most good or the most love?

What defines my life? What's my one thing?

The answers to these questions connect us, or put us in a relationship, to someone or something. The answers ground us. We belong to and we bind our lives to those answers. The twelve apostles knew their one thing.

Today, I've observed that a kind of minimalism exists where religion is concerned, where belonging to a church is tenuous. In my work as an author, catechist, and retreat leader, I meet many Catholics. Their connections to the Catholic Church vary.

Some Catholics lack confidence in God and the Church. They've seen scandals in the Church, and it shakes them. It discourages their willingness to take part in a local church. Even faithful Catholics, who go to Mass every week, may have had negative experiences with some Church members.

For some, belonging to the Church is more of a family tradition, more of a cultural connection; but such belonging does not influence their daily lives. Others are infrequent participants, with one foot in and one foot out. And some Catholics are really former Catholics. They find no close ties to the Church body or her teachings, so they've either moved on to a different church or left church participation entirely. When asked to state a religion on a form or survey, they now list "none."

Some people have a lack of confidence in themselves, too, and that keeps them out of the Church. These folks don't want other people, not to mention God, to know that they don't have it all together. This can be true for all of us. Sometimes bad junk and serious wounds—the worst things we don't ever want to mention—hold us back from mingling with others, especially within a Church setting. We think we're not good enough or too broken or fill-in-the-blank.

My experience tells me that most people yearn for somewhere to put their trust in an unstable world. For some, their seeking comes up empty. Still others are super-focused, and they wind up worshiping or chasing their one thing—only to find out that it is really a lame understudy for God. You name it, and almost anything can be a suitable God-replacement or Church-substitute. The biggest disconnects with God or the Church are usually centered on our own distractions—maybe our preoccupation with and strivings for wealth, power, pleasure, or honor.

So why did I write this book? My one thing, by Mitch and Curly's standards, is my Catholic faith. I'm all in.

When God came first in my life, the rest eventually fell into place and made more sense. I've found a meaningful life in belonging to the Catholic Church, and I'd like to share where I place my trust and why you might be motivated to do the same.

I'm a believer because I found a love that does not disappoint and a lifestyle that challenges me to grow, to overcome vice with virtue. I'm a believer who belongs to a community that trusts in something much more powerful and perfect than our very weak and imperfect selves. I found that I am a better person with these beliefs—and even with those other "church people"—in my life than without.

Belonging matters. Belonging is better than trying to go at life alone. I belong to the Catholic Church and, over time, have learned to trust what she teaches.

REDISCOVER THE MOON

The first time I noticed confident Catholics was when I encountered joyful Catholics. Their spirit and verve attracted me. And this is key to their being all in: their fidelity to Catholicism was fueled by their loving relationship with God.

Jesus Christ was the light of their lives, and belonging to the Church had meaning for them. It is no wonder they were faith-filled Catholics, for Jesus is the true source of all light in the Church. "The Church has no other light than Christ's; according to a favorite image of the Church Fathers, the Church is like the moon, all its light reflected from the sun" (*Catechism of the Catholic Church* [CCC], 748).[1] Ever been enamored with the brightness of the moon on a very dark night? The moon relies on the sun's light. Its sharing in the sunlight is so strong that the light even bounces all the way to earth thousands of miles away. What's impressive is the power source of the sun, not the moon itself. As I was drawn to the light of Christ beaming from the Church members I encountered—true believers—I too found the source of light.

I'm a cradle Catholic. That means I've been a member of the Catholic Church since my infancy, being baptized when I was four weeks old. I trace the seeds of my relationship with Jesus to the foundation given to me by members of my family and by my Catholic-school teachers along the way. Despite being taught about the Catholic faith, I never fully embraced my faith until I was *caught* by the beauty and truth of God's personal love for me.

And then I understood why belonging to the Catholic Church mattered.

Belonging to the Church strengthens and nurtures my relationship with God. It puts me in touch with the lover of my soul, the Beloved One, Jesus.

Belonging to the Church keeps me connected to the conduit of grace, to forgiveness, healing, wisdom, and renewal.

Belonging to the Church connects me to hundreds of brothers and sisters, both on earth and in heaven.

Connections and relationships are at the heart of Catholicism. When it comes to relationships, most people agree that being together is better than being alone. Communion is superior to disunion. Community always outweighs the agony of separation or isolation.

This book discusses our relationship with the Catholic Church, with particular emphasis on how it's where we might place our trust. This book is my answer to the question, What convinces me to be all in?

The idea for this book began to grow several years back when I struggled with disillusionment within the Catholic Church. I worked on staff at a parish when the sex-abuse scandals broke out in the local news implicating many priests in the Roman Catholic Archdiocese of Boston.

For months on end, heartbreak and hysteria swirled like harsh clouds over our heads as disappointment and disgust churned in our minds and hearts. And while I never left the Church, I needed to dig deeper to find reasons to stay faithful.

Over time, for me, the good—the great truths and beauty of the Catholic Church—continued to outshine the bad news in our midst. Years later, I'm daring to write about what I love and why. The Catholic Church, despite warts and flaws that are seen by many, continues to make a positive impact on my life. That is a hope I am willing to share.

Becoming a confident Catholic in the face of negativity, whatever the source, takes time. But to become one—to be all in—means that belonging to the Church really matters to you. The bottom line is, as a Catholic, you either have a relationship with the local Church or you don't.

Our individual relationships to the Church have been uniquely formed by our personal experiences within her. I don't dispute that. You might feel at home in the Church or maybe somewhat uncomfortable. Maybe you are disillusioned or have been hurt. Maybe you don't understand certain teachings, or maybe you disagree with some things certain people have said or done. Maybe you've been a longtime Catholic, but you've never gone deep with God. Maybe you're new to Catholicism and just need some more encouragement. There's a pretty wide continuum when it comes to the experiences of Catholics, so let's find out where we think we stand as we go forward.

Take a little inventory of where you are right now with regard to the Catholic Church. Are you

- deliberately devoted? That is, trying to be a disciple of Jesus?
- dedicated but doing the minimum?
- dabbling or discovering?
- discouraged or done with the Church?

- unsure of where you are?

This book explores what it is to have a relationship with the Church and, by extension, a relationship with God. We cannot discuss one without the other.

As you read along, I hope you'll give yourself permission to explore the themes of each chapter. Allow time to think and reflect on what you can take away from your reading. Take what you need, and use what helps. Do further reading if something interests you.

As you finish each chapter, ask yourself: Where do I stand in relation to the themes presented? In what direction am I moving? Does the reading move me closer to the Church or away? And why?

Our lives are in perpetual motion; even in sleep we are moving as small, imperceptible movements may be happening. The motion of our lives has a trajectory. Ask yourself: Where's my life with the Church leading? Toward communion and relationship? Toward separation and isolation? What movement in my mind and heart do I detect?

The Church is all about communion with Christ and one another. I pray this book might strengthen your confidence as a Catholic and give you a greater appreciation for the richness and treasures of our faith.

I'm often in awe of the saints of the Church; they've seen it *all*—the good, the bad, and the ugly sides of life and the Church through the ages. Their faith never ceases to amaze me. To be a saint is to be all in.

In 2011, our family traveled to Rome for Easter. While visiting St. Peter's Basilica, I spent some time praying before St. John Paul II's tomb. For most of my adult life, I've been inspired by his witness, his preaching, and his writings. John Paul II was declared a saint in 2014. Here's a bit of his wisdom, as we explore our topics:

> God alone is the ultimate basis of all values, of all that is good, noble and true. He is at the beginning

and end of all your questions. He is the answer to life, its probing, its searching. Without reference to God, the world of created values remains in a vacuum. Without reference to him, the world itself remains an unanswered question. . . .

For this reason I invite all of you to "seek first his kingdom and his righteousness" (Mt 6:33). God is love, true love; and his love is alive in you. Reflect that love and those values so that people will say: "I have seen his kingdom," because they have come to know you. . . .

Christ is your friend and he loves you very much. He is your best friend.[2]

St. John Paul II knew his one thing. That one love drove his life. He didn't discover it while driving cattle or driving an MG. He was driven to imitate Christ: to be like the moon—and reflect the Son.

Who or what is driving you?

Pray, Learn, Engage

After each chapter in this book, there will be these three short recommendations for reflection. You can choose to **pray** about the content, **learn** more about the content, or **engage** the content in some concrete fashion.

You can do none, one, two, or all three. There are no quizzes, and nobody is watching. Here are three easy steps to get you started.

Pray

Whenever we are beginning something new, even reading a new book, we can pray and ask for God's help and the grace to do it well. The Holy Spirit is a great helper and giver of aid. Here is a prayer worth memorizing:

> Come, Holy Spirit,
> Fill the hearts of your faithful,
> Enkindle in them the fire of your love.
> Send forth your spirit and we shall be created.
> And you shall renew the face of the earth. Amen.

Learn

At the end of the introduction, a quotation from St. John Paul II made reference to these words of Jesus, his advice on our priorities. They are some of Jesus' most famous words as well as some of the most consoling. See if they have some meaning for you.

> Therefore I tell you, do not worry about your life, what you will eat or what you will drink, or about your body, what you will wear. Is not life more than food, and the body more than clothing? Look at the birds of the air; they neither sow nor reap nor gather into barns, and yet your heavenly Father feeds them. Are you not of more value than they? And can any of you by worrying add a single hour to your span of life? And why do you worry about clothing? Consider the lilies of the field, how they grow; they neither toil nor spin, yet I tell you, even Solomon in all his glory was not clothed like these. But if God so clothes the grass of the field, which is alive today and tomorrow is thrown into the oven, will he not much more clothe you—you of little faith? Therefore do not worry, saying, "What will we eat?" or "What will we drink?" or "What will we wear?" For it is the Gentiles who strive for all these things; and indeed your heavenly Father knows that you need all these things. But *strive first for the kingdom* of God and his righteousness, and all these things will be given to as well. (Mt 6:25–33, emphasis mine)

ENGAGE

Self-assessment can be a healthy thing. The introduction asked the questions below. So if you just glanced over them before, take another moment or two to answer them honestly. With regard to the Catholic Church, are you

- deliberately devoted? A disciple?
- dedicated, but doing the minimum?
- dabbling, or discovering?
- discouraged, or done with the Church?
- unsure of where you are?

Okay, then. Now you know where you stand. You may wish to come back to these questions at the end of the book. In the meantime, I hope you keep reading.

CHAPTER 1

THE BELOVED

THE ONE THING THAT DEFINES US

I pushed open the front door and pulled my coat off, stomping the winter slush from my good leather boots. As my hand came out of the coat sleeve, I could feel the stiff plastic bracelet chafe against my wrist. I can never get those things off. When I first started wearing them at the hospital years ago, they were made of sturdy paper. Now, in the age of hyper-security around patient identification, you either need to be Houdini to slip out of one or have the plastic band cut off.

I walked to the kitchen where I keep the scissors and snipped the patient ID bracelet in half between my name, birthday, and the barcode. Before I pitched the bracelet in the bin, I reminded myself: *this* does not define me.

When scanned by hospital personnel, that plastic band reveals that I belong to the cancer club. If you want to know all the gory details of a middle-aged woman who has survived breast cancer after more than twenty years, just scan that bar code. My medical charts note I've had hip replacements, ankle surgery, vertigo, seasonal allergies, and multiple biopsies. I've struggled with my weight, I've never smoked, and I drink wine regularly. It's all there.

Every physician, nurse, or dentist I've ever met wants to know the cancer story up front. They do the math in their heads—calculating the years between my diagnosis and now. Sometimes I see them wince. Back then I was thirty-six years old, a wife, and a mom of three young children. Fortunately for me, it was caught early. My long-term survivorship and cure is a testament to early intervention, care at a top Boston hospital, and if you ask me, the power of prayer.

After months of exams and multiple surgeries, ultimately, my cancer was declared noninvasive. It did not spread. Yet absolutely *everything else* about becoming a cancer patient *was* invasive, in terms of its impact on my life. Years later, it still is.

Despite an exceptionally full post-cancer life, my original diagnosis never fades from view. For the medical community, it is always their foremost concern. My medical history defines me before they enter the exam room. Yet that little white ID band does not tell the whole story of who I am or what is most important to know about me.

That cancer diagnosis may have been the worst thing that's ever happened to me.

And, you know, we've all got a worst thing. We've all got stuff that we can point to that is the worst—the hurts, the failures, the deaths, the pains, the suffering, the mistakes, the wrongs. Some Catholics call them crosses to bear.

Yet this isn't going to be a book about the negatives in my life. Ultimately, this is about the greatest things, which have gotten me through the worst and are leading me to the best.

BELONGING

More than any other single factor in my life, my belonging to Jesus Christ and the Catholic Church has had the greatest impact on me. Faith gives meaning to everything in my life. It is new eyes to see the world in all its difficulties, or rather, to see *through* all the difficulties with hope as I cling to grace.

Belonging defines me and refines me. Where and in whom I place my trust matters.

Even though I may not always feel like a confident person and I fail and flail on a regular basis, my own frailties do not undermine my confidence in my faith. They provide a catalyst to turn to my faith and to place my trust and hope in the eternal truth and goodness of a God who loves me. God came to save and redeem every frailty, every weakness, every sin, and every broken heart.

That's the first confidence that the Catholic Church offers us: God exists.

And we'll explore a few more: God is real, he loves you, and he invites you to be in his family forever.

My life with Jesus and my confidence in his Church are so much bigger than my medical history. They are even more powerful than my family history, more significant than my work history, and I'm relieved to admit, far greater than my sinful history. My personal history is wrapped up in God's history—his-story, if you will. His-story makes all the difference in mine. My life and yours have great meaning in the arc of eternity.

After fifty-plus years of Catholic life, I've found confidence and hope to be good traveling companions. So may I ask you, dear reader, to offer a little confidence and hope in the journey we'll make in the pages to come? And if you choose to offer a little prayer for this author, while we are engaged here, I wouldn't mind a bit.

CONFIDENCE IN THE BELOVED

I grew up in a churchgoing family. I was taught about God, learned my prayers, and received the sacraments when it was appropriate to do so. I attended Catholic schools, and in sixth grade I made my Confirmation. In the years after my Confirmation, something started to stir within me, spiritually speaking.

Hiking and backpacking highlighted my young teen years; I will never forget standing on a high outcropping of rock and looking out over the Blue Ridge Mountains for the first time. The majesty of that vista touched my girl's heart. Somehow I *knew* that God was with me in that moment of intoxicating beauty. It was as if God broke through the veneer of all my "knowledge" of him that I had been taught and was encountering me. God was somehow talking to me.

I heard no voices, but in that moment, I came to believe that God exists. It was the moment when I began to understand in experience what others had told me about—that God created everything out of love.

That moment seemed timeless. As if time stood still, I became absorbed into something larger than myself. I was connected to it; I participated in it. It was exactly this participation in a thing so beautiful, so totally beyond my own being, that made me ask, Who made such a thing? And I knew who.

God was drawing me toward him by appealing to what was beautiful to my mind and heart. For God is true beauty.

Looking back, that trip planted the seeds for a deeper relationship with God, but the field was plowed by my upbringing. Yet my first mature encounter with God that I can recall was not found in a book or in a church. My first memorable contact with God was in nature. God's beauty in creation won me over—long before I understood the Bible, sacraments, doctrine, or Jesus as my Lord and Savior. Today, I experience all those things as well and am equally awed and inspired by them. But for me, God first used natural beauty to lead me. My heart remembers that every day.

I've since learned to pause and breathe deeply when wonder and awe strike me. It's usually a sign that God's love is somehow at work.

In ensuing years, experiences of beauty kept pointing me to God. While I was climbing trails in the Colorado Rockies, a similar dazzling beauty overtook me. I've also been mesmerized by oceans. The highlight of one recent vacation happened while snorkeling in a coral reef. I came face-to-face with a sea turtle while being surrounded by schools of blue and yellow tangs. Yet none of these beauties of creation captivated my heart like the hours I have spent looking deeply into the eyes of my newborn child. As a mother, I have spent many such moments gazing into the eyes of a tiny soul looking back at me. In all of these encounters, I experienced beauty of a transcendent kind. These amazing wonders could have their existence only in God as a Creator—a proof to me of God's existence.

My mountaintop experiences with God as a teen taught me experientially what the Bible reveals: "For from the greatness and beauty of created things comes a corresponding perception of their Creator" (Ws 13:5). I was discovering what the Catholic Church had long held, that God "can be known with certainty from the created world by the natural light of human reason" (CCC, 36).

My local parish community became the place where the seeds of my young faith in God took root. During my teen years I met those believers I told you about—the joyful ones who really knew God—at a prayer group in my church. They became conduits of God's love for me. They were passionate about being Catholic and excited for me to know God, too. Like people in love, they couldn't help but speak of their beloved. Pope Francis, it seems, would agree: "What kind of love would not feel the need to speak of the beloved, to point him out, to make him known?"[1]

These were confident Catholics I was meeting. They spoke of Jesus with open love of him. It was almost a little embarrassing. I felt I had some pretty good head-knowledge about God but not much heart-knowledge. I knew things *about* God, but I did not *know* God personally. Their passion for Christ was intriguing.

When I was sixteen, I attended a teen retreat weekend held in our parish school. On retreat, we heard talks and songs about the love of Jesus, something I had heard about from those nice folks at the prayer meetings. After lunch we were encouraged to take some quiet time to be alone with God. I found myself walking outside to the ball fields where I had once played church-sponsored softball. I sat on the familiar dugout bench. I had a pocket-sized New Testament next to me given to me by the retreat staff.

I don't remember if I tried to pray or not, but what I remember is that I opened the Bible to a random page. And *whoa*—it was the God-of-the-mountain speaking directly to me:

> For this reason I bow my knees before the Father, from whom every family in heaven and on earth takes its name. I pray that according to the riches of his glory, he may grant that you may be strengthened in your inner being with power through his Spirit, and that Christ may dwell in your hearts through faith, as you are being rooted and grounded in love. I pray that you may have power to comprehend, with all the saints, what is the breadth and length and height and depth, and to know the love of Christ that surpasses knowledge, so that you may be filled with all the fullness of God.
>
> Now to him who by the power at work within us is able to accomplish abundantly far more than all that we ask or imagine, to him be glory in the church and in Christ Jesus to all generations, forever and ever. Amen. (Eph 3:14–21)

The words on the page were alive! In those moments, I found the love that surpasses knowledge. *Zing!* Straight to the heart! There was a stirring inside me, filling me up to know *the breadth, length, height, and depth* of Christ's love for me.

God was there on that bench, the same God from the mountain. I experienced God's fullness that day. And I've been changed by that love ever since. I walked back into that retreat with a new awareness of the realness of God. He knew me. And I *knew* it. I had met the Beloved.

Accepting Jesus' personal love for me defined me. I discovered the honest-to-goodness truth about myself as one who is beloved. I belonged to the Beloved. I belonged to God.

Being beloved is belonging. It is the fruit, the happy fallout, of love. We can't "belove" ourselves. Belovedness is always bestowed as a gift from another.

Can we love ourselves? Yes. Loving ourselves and caring for our well-being are good and noble things. But we are not meant for isolation, we were made for relationships and connection with others. More specifically, we were made for family and made for communion—a big word that evokes deep, intimate contact with another, a beloved one. It also is a deep connectedness with others.

We are designed to be beloved. We know this on a human level. We may have experience being beloved of a parent or grandparent or in a romantic relationship. But we are designed to experience it also on a spiritual level.

We are called to be in a relationship with the true Beloved, Jesus. That's not something we dreamed up on our own. It's not myth or fantasy or wishful thinking. It is God's plan from before the beginning of time. God has always been the initiator when it comes to having relationships with human persons.

GOD LOVED US FIRST

We see God's initiative all through history as we read the Bible. God creates the world and makes human beings—and slowly reveals himself to them, inviting them to know him. Yet that history is fraught with human beings messing things up, not trusting God.

There are so many examples where God initiates powerful and trustworthy relationships, where God is faithful, but the people he chooses are faithful only some of the time and faithless or forgetful at other times. Covenants between God and humans were made and often broken. Yet the breaking part was never God's fault.

God called Abraham, God called Moses, and God called David. All of these great ones sinned. They did not get everything right. Yet God still loved them and had a plan for their lives for their good and the good of others. God patiently loved.

God later called Mary, who accepted the role to become the woman whereby the greatest promise of all would come to pass. God the Son, Jesus, would take on a human body through her, and he would be born to save people from their sins.

Jesus—God's Son and Mary's son—became the perfect man, who finally showed us how to have a relationship with God the Father in heaven, and Jesus traded his life for ours so that we could be free from sins that held us back from God. Jesus made a way for us to live forever with God. In him, all could be united with the God of love.

"'God is Love' and love is his first gift, containing all others" (CCC, 733).

I think of it like this: God created us and promptly fell in love with his creatures. It is not a gooey, heartsick, or sappy kind of love. God desires this union and intimacy with us to bring us everlasting happiness. Since we humans kept messing up our side of the relationship, eventually, God came in person to seal the deal. Jesus came to show us how to live and how to be in a proper relationship with God the Father, the benevolent Creator who created everything and everyone out of love.

God still calls to us today. He often uses other people—especially the people of the Church, such as those who taught me about the faith to prepare my heart, and especially those I met at the retreat when I was older—to point us toward being open to a relationship with God.

God's love for us is a gift. God's love sent Jesus Christ as the way, the truth, and the life for us. And through Jesus Christ, we have the gift of the Holy Spirit, who is guiding the Catholic Church. Through the Church, we have the gift of the Bible and the gifts of the sacraments, and all the graces that God makes available through them, so we can know this truth: God loves us.

God loves you.

God loves me.

It sounds simple, though it's not simplistic. It's profound.

God *is* love.

That's one of the most quoted lines from the Bible, and it's one of the pithiest messages in the world. So much so that it's the stuff of posters, T-shirts, and refrigerator magnets. But do you know who first wrote it? John—an apostle of Jesus and a member of the Early Church. He was one of Jesus' closest friends. John's nickname is "the beloved disciple." The rest of the quotation comes from a letter John wrote to his beloved friends:

> Beloved, let us love one another, because love is from God; everyone who loves is born of God and knows God. . . .
>
> God abides in those who confess that Jesus is the Son of God, and they abide in God. So we have known and believe the love that God has for us.
>
> *God is love,* and those who abide in love abide in God, and God abides in them. Love has been

perfected among us in this: that we may have bold-
ness on the day of judgment, because as he is, so are
we in this world. There is no fear in love, but perfect
love casts out fear; for fear has to do with punish-
ment, and whoever fears has not reached perfection
in love. We love, because he first loved us. (1 Jn 4:7,
15–19, emphasis mine)

God loved us first. That's the starting point for our confidence and hope.

I find it fantastic that the God of the entire universe—
the same God who was paying attention to little ole me
on the mountain and on the dugout bench—waits for our
personal RSVP. God desires us to return that love in freedom, to choose him. And beyond choosing him, he sends
us to love others, allowing our love for him to be expressed
by loving them.

As I got older and read the Bible with more fervor, I
came across a special phrase from Jesus, captured in the
beloved disciple's gospel. When I read it, I remember that
day on the mountain and that afternoon on the bench.

Jesus said to his friends, "You did not choose me but
I chose you" (Jn 15:16). It was Jesus who chose me first.
It was always God's initiative. He was waiting for me to
choose him—to grow in that relationship with him, like
John and Paul, and to become a beloved friend of God,
another beloved disciple.

Something else happened to me that day on the bench
with God. The people on that retreat and in that church
became a family to me. I experienced a connectedness—a
belonging—that I had never understood before. I was no
longer a casual church member taking up a seat in the
pew at church like strangers taking seats in a theater. I
belonged. I was part of the community. God's love connected me to every person in that church. It didn't matter
whether I liked them or not. What mattered was that God
loved them, too.

It was staggering to learn I belonged to something that was much bigger than my little, local church. I was eternally connected to all those believers from throughout history.

St. Paul wrote that God chose us before the world began, that God was thinking of us and dreaming of us before we ever had a clue of his existence: "Blessed be the God and Father of our Lord Jesus Christ, who has blessed us in Christ . . . just as he chose us in Christ before the foundation of the world. . . . He destined us for adoption as his children through Jesus Christ, according to the good pleasure of his will, to the praise of his glorious grace that he freely bestowed on us in the Beloved" (Eph 1:3–6). God the Father that comes through the Beloved Son, Jesus.

It's no coincidence that, throughout the New Testament, the apostles who first loved Jesus called the Early Church members "beloved." Scan the Early Church letters of Peter, Paul, John, James, and Jude, and you'll find this norm. The apostles addressed the followers of Jesus as "beloved." For that is what they were! They were beloved to Christ and therefore to one another.

HOPE IN THE CROSS OF THE BELOVED

It is inspiring to consider that the Beloved, in order to make us beloved, went to the Cross for the sake of love for us. The Bible and the Church teach that Jesus Christ suffered his passion and death on the Cross in atonement for all the sins that had befallen humanity—both before his death and since. That means that Jesus died for you and me.

It is no small thing that Catholics are baptized in the name of the Father, the Son, and the Holy Spirit and marked with the Sign of the Cross. It is at once consoling and slightly ominous when you consider the history the cross has as an instrument for torture and hideous public executions carried out by the ancient Roman government.

The worst criminals were sentenced to be tortured and to hang on a cross to die.

Thanks to the merits of Jesus on the Cross, we have gained so much by his death and resurrection. We have the forgiveness of our sins and the graces of all the sacraments of the Church to benefit us. In and through Christ's resurrection, the Cross has become a true sign of hope and salvation for all people.

When you get right down to it, for our sakes, the Cross is not a negative. It's a plus. Jesus turned something that was excruciating and despicable into something powerfully redemptive.

When I see a cross, or a crucifix with the body of Jesus on it, in my mind I see the death of Jesus, the Son of God, who died there. But with the eyes of faith I see also the victorious side, the plus side. (Maybe I'm crazy, but even the shape of the cross reminds me of a plus sign!) Through something God-awful came something God-inspired.

Since we are called to imitate the Beloved, we too must embrace the Cross in whatever form it takes in our lives. My medical history has been a kind of cross for me for more than twenty years. For you it might be something else. Some crosses, trials, or burdens are short-lived, and some are prolonged.

Our crosses are never overlooked or unseen by the Beloved. This is the God who sees us, knows us—even young girls on mountaintops or ball-field benches. For me, today, God is also the Lord of the pathology lab and the operating table. He can and will accompany us in our worst times if we invite him. Our crosses are not losses when we are joined to Jesus Christ. Even the cruelest crosses that lead to death, when joined to our Beloved, lead to life eternal. That is the hope of the Cross.

Ultimately, God used the Cross of Christ for our good. The same holds for whatever crosses we may struggle with: God can bring something good out of something difficult with his grace. Grace is another way of saying his love can become our divine aid and strength when we need it most.

Over time, I've learned to see the shape of the cross as a symbolic summary of my life—not a negative but a plus. I wonder if this little word picture might be helpful for you as well.

A cross contains both a vertical beam and a horizontal one, and it represents all the relationships in my life. I imagine the vertical beam representing my life between God and me. I visualize God reaching from heaven to earth to invite me to into a relationship and me replying to that in prayer. That vertical dimension is a two-way street. God initiates, and I respond. It also includes the sacrifice that Jesus made for me on the Cross. God came from heaven, took flesh in order to redeem the flesh of a fallen humanity, and raised it up! To thank Jesus for that, I respond to his love for me with my love for him. I pray daily, I go to Sunday Mass, and I find ways to adore and serve Jesus, the Beloved, every day.

I imagine the horizontal beam of the cross as representing my relationships here on earth. Like Jesus' two arms stretched on the Cross, my own arms are meant to stretch to love and embrace others. I respond to the Beloved also by loving the people he has placed in my life: my family, my church, my community. I love them because God first loved me. I have the strength to love them because of the graces God gives me through his love and through the Church.

The vertical and the horizontal parts of my life meet and make sense in Jesus and in the faith that has been passed on to me through the Catholic Church.

I wear a little cross of gold around my neck because, as a Catholic, my life is *both* spiritual *and* religious. I am *both* prayerful interiorly *and*, on the exterior, a practicing Church member trying to live the faith out in the world.

I wear that cross because what happened on Jesus' Cross long ago affects me still. Jesus' love for me, and his sacrifice for me, brings meaning to my everyday life. In him the best of who I am and all my deepest aches meet; the sacred and the stumbling find common ground. In the body and blood of Jesus, given up for me, I have salvation.

I wear that cross because of the faith that was handed down to me by the Church. Without the Catholic Church's influence, born from the blood of the Cross and the power of the Spirit, I would never have been introduced to Jesus Christ. The Church continues to be obedient to Christ's command: "Go therefore and make disciples of all nations" (Mt 28:19). This Church is why I know Jesus and have the promise of heaven.

In Jesus, and in the Church he established, all that is divine is connected to all that is human. And for me, and many others, that changes *everything*. It means there is always *more* to discover, or recover, in everything—it is a finding of the sacred in everyone, in everything, in every day.

I started this chapter telling you that cancer does not have the last word in my life. The arc of gratitude from then to now is sometimes hard to explain. Cancer, in some ways, refocused everything I needed to know about being beloved of God, and it led me to embrace everything that was important in life and in death. I realized just how great life *really is*—how happy I was, and what a gift every single year is, every month, every day, and *heck*, every breath.

I've lived to see and to believe what the beloved disciple once wrote about Jesus: "From his fullness we have all received, grace upon grace" (Jn 1:16). From the fullness of a life in Christ, we receive more than we could ask for or imagine—"*grace upon grace.*"

Did cancer have an enduring impact on me? Sure it did. But there are so many things more powerful than cancer. You want to talk about impact of a greater magnitude?

It's a living faith, an ongoing encounter with Christ. I find it in my prayerful relationship with Jesus, in my personal relationships with those I live and work with, and in my passionate embrace of the Catholic Church.

I'm a work in progress, but while I'm working on it, I'm going all in. I know I don't have it all together—I thank God that the Church teaches about *ongoing* conversion. But I've been taking notes for a long time on what moves me and what changes me for the better. Those notes will be making up the rest of this book. I'll be sharing what makes me confident about being a Catholic and how the Church and what she teaches benefits my life.

All I've learned about Jesus and about having the fullness of life in him comes from the wisdom of the Church. We're all called to experience *grace upon grace*—to be beloved disciples.

To become all in, we've got to see what's worth dying for, as Jesus did. Jesus died for us. We've got to be convinced of the truth, the goodness, and the beauty of our inherent belovedness, of our belonging to him, such that he would die for us.

Belonging to Jesus matters. Belonging to the Church matters. "In the Church, God is 'calling together' his people from all the ends of the earth. The equivalent Greek term *Kyriake*, from which the English word *Church* . . . [is] derived, means *'what belongs to the Lord'*" (CCC, 751; emphasis mine).

Who and what we belong to matters.

PRAY

Meditation is a form of prayer that engages our minds and hearts as we ponder a holy message, such as praying over and pondering the words of scripture. You might want to start by praying the prayer to the Holy Spirit, found at the end of the introduction. Then read the following verse a few times slowly to get the sense of it. Then rest with it and see what God might be saying to you through it.

Take ten minutes and meditate on this verse from the beloved disciple, John: "God is love, and those who abide in love abide in God, and God abides in them" (1 Jn 4:16).

LEARN

Using a Bible or an Internet search engine, have some fun looking up and finding in scripture the word *beloved*— used as a term of endearment by the members of the Early Church (and to underscore the truth that they believed about one another). There's a sample list of verses below. You don't have to do them all, but you might wish to come back to this list if you have time later. Choose a few of these New Testament scripture verses to get started:

Romans 1:7; 12:19; 16:5; 16:8–9; 16:12

1 Corinthians 4:14; 4:17; 10:14; 15:58

2 Corinthians 7:1; 12:19

Ephesians 1:6; 5:1; 6:21

Philippians 2:12; 4:1

Colossians 1:7; 4:7; 4:9; 4:14

1 Thessalonians 1:4

2 Thessalonians 2:13

2 Timothy 1:2

Philemon 1:1; 1:16

Hebrews 6:9

James 1:16; 1:19; 2:5

1 Peter 2:11; 4:12

2 Peter 3:1; 3:8; 3:14–15; 3:17

1 John 2:7; 3:2; 3:21; 4:1; 4:7; 4:11

3 John 1:1–2; 1:5; 1:11

Jude 1:1; 1:3; 1:17; 1:20

Note: For Catholics, the following biblical translations are recommended: *New Revised Standard Version, Catholic Edition* (NRSVCE); or *New American Bible, Revised Edition* (NABRE).

ENGAGE

This is an exercise that builds our awareness of God. Find a small cross (or trace a cross on a small object), and carry it in your pocket or purse. Let the cross remind you of Jesus. For the next twenty-four hours, keep it on your person, in your workspace, or where you relax so you will see it all day long. Keep it with you wherever you are, wherever you go. Try to be mindful of that little cross (that is, be mindful of Jesus) for twenty-four hours. (For most of us, this is very hard to do.)

Let this exercise remind you that you are always on Jesus' mind even if you are not always mindful of him. Jesus had you in mind when he carried his Cross. You are beloved.

CHAPTER 2

God's Love Made Visible

Yuck! A Mud-Splashed Bride!

I love the coffee at the cozy restaurant just a short walk from our church parking lot. A woman from the Bible study I was leading asked to talk to me outside of class, and we met at that restaurant. She was my lunch companion that day. As I munched my salad, I listened to her rail about disparaging news items about the Catholic Church—the latest in a string of disappointments for her. I understand how these things can be setbacks to a person's faith. Negative press always brings fallout. Bad news about the Church can shake even churchgoing Catholics like this good woman. For some it drives them to make a choice—to lean into or away from the Church. My lunch date's confidence in the Church was shrinking.

I didn't know that afternoon that my friend was seriously thinking about stepping away from the Church. I'm glad I prayed before we met because it allowed me to listen to the state of her heart and not to get caught up in taking sides in the politics of the news item. This woman, a convert to Catholicism years ago and endowed with very strong intellectual gifts, was clearly rattled. I perceived a tear behind her glasses.

One thing was very clear as she spoke: she had great faith in Jesus Christ, but her faith in the institution of the Church was eroding. She was seriously questioning the current leadership of those mentioned in the news accounts. She wanted to know how I dealt with these things without falling apart or losing my faith.

I finished my coffee and tried to smile in reassurance before I gave my answer. In the post-scandal years, I've had many such conversations. I'm no stranger to disappointment in the Catholic Church either.

My experience taught me that sometimes all we can see of the Church are the imperfections and sins that sully it. Many of us have experienced the flawed humanity of the institution of the Church, the sinful and stumbling members of the Church. And while I agree that some members are unprincipled and lacking in integrity, there are many more good and holy priests and members of the laity.

As a cradle Catholic in midlife, I've had my fair share of dealing with the flaws, shortcomings, and outright poor conduct of Catholics and Church authorities I've known. There's only so much that can be excused in the name of immaturity or people not knowing any better. At times, there is some downright bad behavior going on and, in certain instances, humiliating and criminal behavior.

Sadly, some of my loved ones have been victimized by the actions of bad Catholics and even by unholy priests. Heart-piercing sins from within the Church have hurt my family and friends. Yet I'm not here to make this a lurid tell-all. No doubt, if you're a Catholic over the age of eight and you can read a newspaper or listen to the media, you've been affected, too.

Shocking scandals—be it the clergy sexual-abuse cases, reports of fiscal malfeasance, bickering Church members, poor pastoring damaging the faith, or you name it—all have brought disillusionment and pure revulsion to those still occupying the pews as well as the oh-so-many who have left. There's plenty of hurt to go around whether you consider yourself inside or outside the Catholic Church.

It is not just scandals muddying the Church from within that drives Catholics away. People are making the choice to leave because the culture today offers a plethora of alternatives outside their religion that compete for their attentions and affections. People make value judgments every day on how they are going to spend their time, their money, and their love. Too often the Church just doesn't make the cut. So people walk away from the Church because they deem it irrelevant to their lives.

Many suffer a tremendous lack of confidence in the Church. It's a global problem, this leave-taking, but it's also a personal one for you and me who are left to choose.

I understand the questions that come from Catholics who remain, from Catholics who may be considering trying to return to the Church after being away, or from future would-be converts.

How does one stand with a Church that may seem, at times, very unlovable or at odds with and even disconnected from the culture?

How does one belong when members seem to be fading away because of the Church's lack of popularity or, worse, because of her being discredited by the actions of some of her own people, including priests and bishops?

Why bother? Why belong? What good is it?

I've had to dig down deep to answer for myself why belonging to the Catholic Church matters. There are many benefits just as there is much goodness in the Church's people, priests, and teachings. I know because I cling to this faith and this Church despite adverse conditions.

Let me offer one truth that has proved stabilizing for me, an anchor amid storms and scandals: the Catholic

Church is the Bride of Christ. That means that Jesus, who is God, the second person of the Trinity, is the Bridegroom.

This is a fantastic idea! And yet, in light of the negativity toward Catholicism, if this Church is the Bride, many think she needs one heck of a makeover!

From my vantage point, many people view the Church as a mud-splashed bride. For some, what was once beautiful cannot be appreciated because the soil of hard times has taken its toll. Sometimes, there's so much pain that we've experienced that it's hard to see or feel differently. We fail to see the truth of the Bride's beauty and her best potential. It may seem easier to write her off and cut our losses.

Yet.

Yet there exists, in reality, a holy marriage between the two, between the Bridegroom, Jesus, and his Bride, the Church.

And to date, there has been no divorce. And there never will be.

What?

I mean that this idea of bride and bridegroom is more than an analogy or just some nice metaphor or platitude. This coming together of God and his people is in the great big plan that God decided on long ago. We'll come back to that plan in a little while. For now, back to the Bridegroom.

From its earliest days, the Catholic Church has taught that Jesus is the Bridegroom and we, the Church, are his Bride. St. Paul, in the first century, wrote, "'For this reason a man will leave his father and mother and be joined to his wife, and the two will become one flesh.' This is a great mystery, and I am applying it to Christ and the church" (Eph 5:31–32).

The Catholic Church, in recent years, has been the subject of scandals and difficulties across the globe. I won't minimize that.

Yet. No matter how battered your opinion or my opinion of the global or local Church might be at times, "Christ loves the Church as His bride."[1] The opinion of Jesus Christ matters most. And the Church is *still* his Bride.

ANOTHER TIME, ANOTHER PLACE, ANOTHER BRIDE AND GROOM

A phrase from my wedding invitation has stayed with me for more than thirty years. I was planning a wedding about the same time that I was a struggling copywriter in radio. Being the wordsmithy bride-to-be, it fell to me to compose our wedding invitations, alongside my soon-to-be groom. Besides the announcement of the names, dates, times, and places that most invitations have, there is usually precious little space for any further sentiment. However, we managed to add a phrase that helped us relate the meaning that the day had for us.

The invitation was addressed from our parents, and it read, in part:

> You are invited to celebrate
> *the gift of God's love made visible*
> when
> Patricia and Robert
> become united in one as Christ
> in the holy sacrament of Matrimony. . . .

Since that tender time, I've had decades to consider what *the gift of God's love made visible* really means in my life. It meant one thing for my marriage, in terms of the unity of husband and wife and our unity with God. But *the gift of God's love made visible* has been manifest in so many other ways.

God's love became visible to me—became tangibly real—not only through that retreat in my teen years but in ongoing ways: through God's voice in the Bible, the graces I received in the sacraments, and the people in our parish faith community that surrounded me. But for me, God used my marriage to profoundly shape my understanding of his love.

A little history: as a young woman grappling with living her Catholic faith, I became friends with a young man trying to do the same. This would be my future husband, Bob. He was a devout Catholic, and we dated while we were in college. Our common Catholic vision played a strong role in our deciding on marriage in the Church. We believed back then, and still do today, that God loved us. And that it was not only our idea but also God's idea that we should marry.

We trusted what Archbishop Fulton J. Sheen had famously preached years ago, that it takes *three* to get married: God, plus the couple. Even in those younger years, we believed that our marriage was a gift from God to us. Our gift to God in return was the hope that God might allow us to make his love visible on earth. The love we shared in our family was to be a sign of God's love to our three children, to our neighbors, to our parish, and to whomever we met in the world.

It is a profound idea that God entrusts human persons to bring his love to others—because we can really mess it up! God takes a big risk putting us in charge of making his love visible. For the record, Bob and I often failed miserably at loving one another and our family. Everyone makes mistakes in family life, and some learning curves are steeper than others. Yet failure is rarely a permanent state. We held on to hope and forgiveness and asked in prayer for graces to aid us in doing better and in trying to heal hurts along the way.

The vows of marriage, in their own way, make the gift of God's love visible as they remind us of loyalty and faithfulness, "in sickness and in health, for richer and for poorer, in good times and in bad." They really are a vow to try to love like God loves because God's love is constant and everlasting. Through the years we learned to love with great fidelity and to understand what St. Peter meant when he said, "Above all, maintain constant love for one another, for love covers a multitude of sins" (1 Pt 4:8).

I've never forgotten those words on the wedding invitation, and as I look back, they became a foundation for our married life. Yet it was not until later that I learned that this gift of God's love being made visible in my marriage was a microcosm of something much more vast and cosmic.

The invisible God is all about making his love visible. In the Nicene Creed that Catholics profess at Mass, we pray:

> I believe in one God,
> the Father almighty,
> maker of heaven and earth,
> of all things visible and invisible.

This prayer declares belief in an almighty God, identified as a Father who created all things, including us.

God has been slowly revealing his love through the ages—making his love visible through his gift of creation and especially through the creation of human persons. The interesting part is this: a perfect, invisible, and all-powerful God really has no need of us at all. He is perfectly perfect in his perfect and blessed life. There is no other reason for God to create us other than love.

The first sentence of the *Catechism of the Catholic Church* captures it perfectly: "God, infinitely perfect and blessed in himself, in a plan of sheer goodness freely created man to make him share in his own blessed life" (*CCC*, 1).

God has no need of human persons; he's God. Yet God found ways to speak to human hearts. St. Bernard mused on God's decision to reveal himself to us. It seems the almighty, invisible, omnipotent, omnipresent, and everlasting God wished to be *known*. "What concept could man have of God if he did not first fashion an image of him in his heart? By nature incomprehensible and inaccessible, he was invisible and unthinkable, but now he wished to be understood, to be seen and thought of."[2] Imagine that: God wanted to be thought of by you and me. This is another fantastic idea!

In the Bible, we find when God first created human persons, he desired conversations with them. God wanted to be in relationship with his creatures even though he was above them in all ways.

The history of God's plan of love for us is captured in the Bible. The important history of the Old Testament set the stage for God's revelation of himself. The invisible God was revealing himself and his love more and more using people and creation.

God's communication often occurred with a few chosen individuals such as Abraham and Moses and others such as his prophets and some faithful kings. God readily used created things, too, to get his messages across. We think of his voice coming through the burning bush, a pillar of cloud, and a great sea parting. God also entered into covenants that built bonds of relationship between himself and the Chosen People, Israel.

For many, many centuries, God's Chosen People believed in this invisible God and worshiped him. And they also messed up a lot. I can so relate! They sinned and broke the relationship with God. They would reject God, then God would help bring restoration, things would get better, and then the sin cycle would happen again.

God's plan of sheer goodness seems a pretty bumpy ride if you ask me. But the trouble usually comes from the human side of the relationship, not the divine side. God never stopped loving us from his side!

St. Gregory of Nyssa describes the love that moved God to action: "Sick, our nature demanded to be healed; fallen, to be raised up; dead, to rise again. We had lost the possession of the good; it was necessary for it to be given back to us. Closed in the darkness, it was necessary to bring us the light; captives, we awaited a Savior; prisoners, help; slaves, a liberator. Are these things minor or insignificant? Did they not move God to descend to human nature and visit it, since humanity was in so miserable and unhappy a state?"[3] God's plan of sheer goodness held a secret remedy. The most powerful gift of God's love made visible was in the coming of his very self to redeem us.

The gift of God's love made visible is another way of describing the *Incarnation*. That's a big churchy word, but it's important to ask: What is the Incarnation? It is the fact that Jesus Christ, the Son of God—yes, God himself!—took on a human nature and became a man "in order to accomplish our salvation in the same human nature."[4] The Catholic Church confidently professes that Jesus Christ, the second person of the Trinity is "both true God and true man, not part God and part man."[5]

Jesus Christ is both God and man. God stooped to be joined with his creation. He stepped out of the realm of heaven—his perfect and blessed life—and entered our world of brokenness, messiness, and sin. Not only that but God would use the very human nature of Jesus to save us. And it was no small thing.

So back to lunch with my friend who was wondering what I would say to the latest Church woes found in the news.

My first reaction: *Prayer. And then, more prayer.* We all need to pray for the Church on earth. My friend was praying regularly, indeed. Her faith in Jesus was unshakable. But all these church people were really mucking things up.

So we started with talking about Jesus and who he really is as God and man. The Incarnation of Christ is fundamental to Christianity. "Belief in the true Incarnation of the Son of God is the distinctive sign of Christian faith: 'By this you know the Spirit of God: every spirit which confesses that Jesus Christ has come in the flesh is of God' [1 Jn 4:2]. Such is the joyous conviction of the Church from her beginning whenever she sings 'the mystery of our religion': 'He was manifested in the flesh' [1 Tm 3:16]" (*CCC*, 463).

The Incarnation is the antidote for what I call the "mud-splashed-bride syndrome."

Recall what Jesus taught about the bride and bridegroom in marriage: "'The two shall become one flesh.' . . . They are no longer two, but one flesh. Therefore what God has joined together, let no one separate" (Mk 10:8–9).

Remember this idea: what God has joined together, we must not divide. It will come in handy later in this book.

Not only is Jesus both divine and human, for what God has joined will never be separated, but Christ will never be separated from his Bride for the same reason. "It is in the Church that Christ fulfills and reveals his own mystery as the purpose of God's plan: 'to unite all things in him' [Eph 1:10]. St. Paul calls the nuptial union of Christ and the Church 'a great mystery' [Eph 5:32]. Because she is united to Christ as to her bridegroom, she becomes a mystery in her turn. Contemplating this mystery in her, Paul exclaims: 'Christ in you, the hope of glory' [Col 1:27]"(*CCC*, 772). Jesus and the Church are one. Therefore, we can also say that because the Church is wedded to Jesus, the Church is both human and divine.

I explained this that day at the lunch table. Just as Jesus is human and divine, so is the Church. The Church can be both—*is* both—just as Jesus is both. My distressed friend was greatly consoled. No one had ever explained to her the nature of the Church as being human *and* divine.

The Incarnation of Christ changes everything.

Jesus is the gift of God's love made visible.

And guess what? So is the Church. Everything that Jesus is he pours into the Church. The Church, thanks to

Jesus, is a radiant Bride, resplendent with graces. She offers access to the treasures—the glory—that heaven can bring to earth through her.

Yes, I'm talking about that same blessedly human institution whose followers do not always live up to their true radiance as Bride. Nonetheless, that is what they are.

The Church is the beloved of Jesus.

The unity of Jesus and the Church is a merciful truth that far outweighs the sins of the Bride, who is forgiven when she repents. (That's not to say the members of churches are not liable for crimes and misdemeanors within a civil system; her guilty members most certainly are liable.) But *in Christ*, who is always present, there is always the hope of *glory* for the Bride. Hers is an ever-present forgiveness and mercy both to dispense and to receive. The Church knows that Jesus, who is God, is her divine strength, even as her human members are often weak, sinful, or foolish.

The Church acknowledges that just as Jesus' mission on earth was fraught with difficulties, persecution, and peril, so is hers. Jesus came to embrace sinners, though holy and innocent himself. The Church, too, embraces sinners, while at the same time the Church knows she lives in a both/and situation. The Church lives in both "the now" and "the not yet," what is and what is to come. "It is of the essence of the Church that she be both human and divine, visible and yet invisibly equipped . . . present in this world and yet not at home in it."[6]

The Church, being wedded to Christ, is *both* human *and* divine. The Second Vatican Council described this as the Church being both "holy and always in need of being purified, always follow[ing] the way of penance and renewal."[7]

The Church's divinity looks a lot like Christ in his divinity. In the Church we find and worship God Incarnate, who redeems us and offers the promise of heaven.

In the Church dwells all manner of truth, goodness, and beauty.

The Church's humanity looks a lot like us. We might hope and aspire to be holy and good, yet we are always, *always*, in need of renewal and forgiveness. And that's stating it mildly, right? Yet the Church that we see visibly is also invisibly equipped—her source of power is in the Beloved who came from heaven in search of her, and who longs for her to make her home with him there.

At her best, the humanity of the Church can resemble the humanity of Jesus, the one who showed us the best way to live and love. "The Church, 'like a stranger in a foreign land, presses forward amid the persecutions of the world and the consolations of God' [cf. Gal 4:6; Rom 8:15–16, 26], announcing the cross and death of the Lord 'until he comes.' By the power of the risen Lord it is given strength that it might, in patience and in love, overcome its sorrows and its challenges, both within itself and from without, and that it might reveal to the world, faithfully though darkly, the mystery of its Lord until, in the end, it will be manifested in full light."[8] The full light we seek is heaven; our hope in Christ tells us it is there, waiting for us in the distance.

The Church is a bride on a journey who cannot wait to get to the great wedding banquet that will happen in heaven. Yet along the way she keeps inviting new guests to the party. Not all of them are ready for such festivities or fully appreciate her invitation, but they are walking along with her. A bride walking along a long road in all seasons is likely to get mud on her dress. It's inevitable.

Until we reach heaven, our experience with the Church may test our fidelity to Christ and, through him, our fidelity to one another. Until we get to the bliss of heaven, much of what we experience in the Church may look a lot like the up-and-down, back-and-forth seasons of marriage: "in sickness and in health, for richer and for poorer, in good times and in bad."

Even popes have to deal with scandals and how they affect our belief and trust in the Church! In recent years, Pope Benedict XVI expressed amazement at Christ's fidelity to us in the face of the infidelity of many Church members.

> Right now, in the midst of the scandals, we have experienced what it means to be very stunned by how wretched the Church is, by how much her members fail to follow Christ. That is the one side, which we are forced to experience for our humiliation, for our real humility. The other side is that, in spite of everything, [Jesus] does not release his grip on the Church. In spite of the weakness of the people to whom he shows himself, he keeps the Church in his grasp, he raises up saints in her, and makes himself present through them. I believe that these two feelings belong together: the deep shock over the wretchedness, the sinfulness of the Church—and the deep shock over the fact that he doesn't drop this instrument, but that he works with it; that he never ceases to show himself through and in the Church.[9]

This much is certain: our hope is always in Jesus, the Beloved. And we will need grace to help our love stay secure. Fortunately, that is something that is in great supply.

Jesus is permanently wedded to the Church, his Bride. Jesus is the founder of the Church, the keeper of the Church, and the Bridegroom of the Church. The future of the Church belongs to Jesus alone. That's the big picture.

The life and love of Jesus is wedded with the Church no matter what. His words were, "I am with you always"

(Mt 28:20). Jesus is the faithful Bridegroom. His Incarnation—his becoming one of us to become one with us—makes all the difference. It's a prime reason I'm a confident Catholic.

With Jesus as the Bridegroom, I'm all in.

PRAY

As in chapter 1, meditate on the Incarnation of Jesus, whom the beloved disciple describes as "the Word [who] became flesh" (Jn 1:14). Ask the Holy Spirit to guide you. Using a Bible, meditate for ten minutes on John 1:1–14, 16.

LEARN

Read more about Jesus' Incarnation in the *Catechism of the Catholic Church*, 461–483. If you don't have a print copy, you can find online versions. See the resources listed in the back of this book. (When you're reading the *Catechism*, keep in mind that, as with most Church documents, the numbers cited are not page numbers but paragraph numbers.)

ENGAGE

If you are married, try one of these options:

- Find your wedding invitation or marriage license. As you reminisce, offer a prayer thanking God for your beloved spouse. Then write him or her a love note.
- Read the Song of Songs in the Bible.

If you are not married, try one of these options:

- Pick a married couple you know or one of the married couples on CatholicMatch.com and offer prayers for them. (See http://www.catholicmatch.com/about/category/success-stories/.)
- Read the Song of Songs in the Bible.

If you are discerning the vocation to marriage, consider reading the Christian classic *Three to Get Married* by Archbishop Fulton J. Sheen.

CHAPTER 3

CONFIDENCE IN GOD'S PLAN

WITHOUT THE CHURCH THERE IS NO CHRISTMAS

Christmas, for many, is forever joined to December 25. We don't question it, and we could never forget it. We Catholics celebrate it—the Church has kept its truth alive for more than two thousand years. Christmas can never be just an ordinary day.

We love the Christmas story. Read the first and second chapters of Matthew's or Luke's gospel. We love the drama of God speaking through an angel, asking a young maiden to bear his Son. We are moved by the faith of a young couple traveling to Bethlehem: the wife expecting a baby any moment and the husband searching for a place of rest and comfort for his wife to give birth.

The baby is a special one—the long-awaited Messiah from the kingly line of David who will save his people, Israel. Eventually the news of this Messiah will reach beyond the Chosen People of Israel to the whole world!

Alas, in the meantime, this little king's nobility is overshadowed by his family's poverty. He is born amid the warmth and comfort of his parents' love but given a humble straw bed in a feed trough. Yet heaven did not

overlook his kingly coming. Outside, the sky is adorned
with a remarkable star. A supernatural choir of singing
angels greets Jesus' arrival. The angels announce the birth
of this precious Savior—the one who would later call himself the Good Shepherd—to local shepherds tending sheep
in a nearby pastureland.

> The angel said to them, "Do not be afraid; for see—I
> am bringing you good news of great joy for all the
> people: to you is born this day in the city of David a
> Savior, who is the Messiah, the Lord. This will be a
> sign for you: you will find a child wrapped in bands
> of cloth and lying in a manger." And suddenly there
> was with the angel a multitude of the heavenly host,
> praising God and saying,
>
> > "Glory to God in the highest heaven,
> >   and on earth peace among those whom he
> > favors!" (Lk 2:10–14)

What God had joined together was remarkable. The
world would never be the same. Heaven and earth were
joined in the birth of the Savior. The Son of God became
the son of Mary and the foster child of Joseph.

God had come to earth.

God joined himself to humanity—and took on human
skin and bones and blood and DNA—in order to save it.
What God has joined, we must not divide.

Yet so often, in our minds and hearts, we divide God
from his great works or his truth from our reality. The truth
of Christmas can be obscured by distractions we deem
more important. We can separate Christmas from Jesus
unwittingly by playing up gift giving and holiday reveling
as more important than the religious feast it is. Or we pay
more attention to children and stories of Santa Claus than
to the true story of the Christ Child who brings true joy.

I'm not criticizing the true story of St. Nicholas or
even his cultural reinventions as Kris Kringle or Santa

Claus. What I'm getting at is the fact that we often choose to replace the central focus of Christmas with lesser emphases. The same happens, culturally, with Easter. But I digress.

We unwittingly, or sometimes on purpose, separate what God has joined.

I remember a night during my childhood when I unexpectedly ran headlong into truth rather than fiction. As a child, much of my sense of Christmas was focused on what gifts would be mine under the Christmas tree. My parents never made a big deal about the tradition regarding Santa Claus. But my school pals sure did! It was hard to know what to believe! Somewhere around the second grade, I became aware that my parents were impersonating St. Nicholas. It came as a slow-motion shock one Christmas Eve.

Long after my sisters and I had been tucked into bed, happily anticipating Christmas morning, I was suddenly jolted awake by a nasty stomach flu. My malady necessitated that I make several trips to the bathroom that night. After each episode, my mother quietly herded me back to bed. Over the course of multiple awakenings, I witnessed my parents slowly filling our stockings and laying gifts under the tree. I eventually fell asleep till morning. Yet I awoke with the big-kid realization that Christmas was not all about a jolly elf with a sleigh or fulfillment of my wish list for "St. Nick."

This little memory reminds me of the truth that things aren't always what they seem. In fact, they are often better than we expect. That Christmas I learned that it was not a stranger elf in a red suit who somehow saw me from far away and made a judgment call on my worthiness. No, indeed, it was the people who knew me and really loved me the most who bore the gifts at Christmas.

Wouldn't we really rather receive gifts from those who love us the most?

Who the giver is makes all the difference in how we receive the gift.

Of course, this taps into the very heart of the Christmas story. The Father in heaven—the giver of all good things—sends his Son to earth. The Son willingly embodies the love of the Father, becoming the greatest gift in the greatest story ever told.

As I matured and learned the depth of the real Christmas story, the Nativity scene came to life for me. The stuff of Christmas—the gift giving, the tree, the carols, the baking, the fun—all played a supporting role to the true star and attraction of Christmas: Jesus.

Christmas Day is Jesus' birthday—but we're the ones who get the Gift.

As the years rolled along, I became a parent myself. I deeply understood the sacrifices parents make for their children. They hope and dream for their children's happiness. The Christmas narrative took on a much more important dimension for me once I became a parent. It became easier to envision that in God we have a Father who is concerned with his children's happiness and well-being. This same God sent his Beloved Son to live among us.

Liturgically, for Catholics, the Incarnation is celebrated on March 25, on the Solemnity of the Annunciation of the Lord, when Jesus took flesh in Mary's womb. Yet in practice, for many people, Christmas Day is the visible celebration of the Incarnation—the Nativity, or birth, of Jesus Christ, the second person of the Blessed Trinity. In this amazing yet true story, the Son of God—the omnipotent, omniscient, almighty, and ever-living God—foregoes heaven's throne to enter human existence as a babe in a manger.

The Son of God came for a reason: to complete the plan and not just any plan—the plan of God, the plan that flows from the God who is love.

This is the plan that the Church willingly proclaims. For the Church has a role in that plan. Recently Pope Francis preached that the Church is a love story. "The Church begins . . . in the heart of the Father, who had this idea . . . of love. So this love story began, a story that has gone on for so long, and is not yet ended. We, the women and men of the Church, we are in the middle of a love story: each of us is a link in this chain of love. And if we do not understand this, we have understood nothing of what the Church is."[1]

The Church, if I may echo Francis, is not a mushroom that sprung up on its own; she is not a man-made entity. She existed in the heart of the Father, within the Trinity, until the time was right for the Father to send his Son who established her on earth.

We are part of this love story of God, the unfolding of his plan.

God's innermost secret is that he is love. And God's love is the centerpiece of the Trinity and of the Church. This love story spills out of God's eternity into history. We experience God's coming to us—indeed, that this love story now involves us—profoundly at Christmastime.

> A virgin conceived, bore a son, and yet remained a virgin. This is no common occurrence, but a sign; no reason here but God's power, for he is the cause, and not nature. It is a special event, not shared with others; it is divine, not human. Christ's birth was not necessity, but an expression of omnipotence . . . for the redemption of men. . . . That the Creator is in his creature and God is in the flesh brings dignity to man without dishonor to him who made him. . . .
>
> He has made you in his image that you might in your person make the invisible Creator present on earth.[2]

WHAT GOD HAS JOINED . . .

Recall how the Church is the Bride of Christ. She is also the great keeper of the story of salvation, which tells how God created the heavens and the earth, how the first humans sinned, and about the subsequent fall of humanity. But for love of us, God longed to save humanity. God, the author of life, the same God, would join himself to humanity—he would become one of us.

And what God had joined, we must not divide.

We're now familiar with the marriage context of Jesus' words "what God has joined together, let no one separate." Let's take those same words of Jesus and apply them to the broader context of God's plan for human life in the universe.

Let's take, for example, human life's dependence on oxygen. God, as the earth's creator, has joined earth to an atmosphere to promote the life of many species of plants and animals but most especially human life. We live in an oxygenated ecosystem designed by God to sustain human life. When humans are separated from earth's atmosphere in space travel, they need an artificial atmosphere, a form of life support in their spacecraft and space suits; otherwise, the astronauts will die.

Another example can be found in the intricate design of a woman's body, capable of bearing new human life. For centuries biological studies have marveled at the miracle of the creative powers found within masculinity and femininity. When egg and sperm are released and joined in an act of sexual intercourse, a child is conceived. A woman's healthy body is exactly and expertly designed to care for that child, in most cases, until the child is birthed. To prematurely separate what God has joined, to separate a developing embryo from its mother, is to bring harm to that child and to the mother's well-being.

What God has joined together, we must not separate. God's ideas are not ours; his ways are not ours.

The Incarnation of Christ is the game changer.

The Incarnation is when Jesus—who is God, the second person of the Trinity—took on human flesh and became a man. God joins the human race to become one with his creation. In the most intimate way possible, God becomes one with us. Here we could also say, again, that what God has joined, we must not divide.

Even when the people of Jesus' time put him to death, God did not reject humanity.

The Resurrection proves that what God had joined together—himself and human nature—is truly a most glorious thing, and he proposes it to be so for eternity. Even death could not separate God from his creation. Jesus now has a glorified human body in heaven.

God means to be joined *to us* for all time. He has made provision in himself so that we can be in union with God and all the saints in heaven. In the Incarnation, Jesus joined himself to us, not only to accomplish his mission while on earth but also to pave the way for our entrance to live with him one day in heaven, when we will have risen, glorified bodies.

Jesus, once born as a baby in a manger, now reigns in heaven with a risen body. He is our risen Lord, raised up never to die again.

Here's my point, and I bet you can hear it in your mind: what God has joined, we must not divide.

GOD IS JOINED TO WORD AND SACRAMENT

God has joined himself to the Church as a bridegroom is joined in marriage to a bride. We've already covered this, but it is worthy of further treatment.

Jesus will never divorce the Church. Jesus is permanently wedded to the Church. What is Christ's is the Church's, and all that the Church has comes from his merits, glory, power, and magnificent love.

St. Leo the Great taught "what was visible in our Savior has passed over into his mysteries" (CCC, 1115). Those Christian mysteries are the seven sacraments of the Church: Baptism, Confirmation, Eucharist, Penance, the Anointing of the Sick, Matrimony, and Holy Orders.

If Christ is divine then he shares that divine life with the Church. If Christ is human, he shares his humanity with the Church. The Church is never just one or the other. She is always both at the same time. She is always both/and. The Church is both human and divine because God joined himself—the God-man—to the Church.

Sometimes we mistakenly believe that the Church is divine because of God and that it is human because of us. That's only part of the story. She is human and divine because God joined himself to her. Let us not separate what God has joined together.

God joined himself to us to share his divine life with us in part now and in full in heaven.

Consider that almighty God is, indeed, above his creation in his majesty, yet God willingly joins himself to his creation, thanks to the Incarnation. He does so in order to meet with us, to communicate with us, that we may enjoy a closer relationship with him.

Think of how this principle operates in the Church: God joins himself to us through word and sacrament.

Catholics believe that sacred scripture is the inspired Word of God. God dwells in his word, and his word is power. John's gospel declares about the Incarnation: "And the Word became flesh and lived among us, and we have seen his glory, the glory of a father's only son, full of grace and truth" (Jn 1:14).

God also binds his love and powers to the graces found in the sacraments. The sacraments contain God's glory; that is, they are filled with his magnificent love for us and graces to strengthen us. That is why the Catholic Church, to this day, stands behind the indissolubility of the sacrament of Matrimony. The graces of that sacrament are a participation in the divine life of Christ and help married couples to live their vocational call in and through their vows. When couples separate their life from God and one another, selfishness takes over and many marriages fail.

Here are a couple more sacramental examples.

God joins himself to us personally through Baptism. What God has joined together, we must not divide. God baptizes us and makes us his children. When we separate ourselves from that reality, we can lose our sense of identity. Being a beloved child of God is our single greatest identity, which sheds light on everything we are and all we do.

When we disassociate from our baptisms, or when we fail to live the promises of our baptisms, we step away from the family of God, the Church. We divide ourselves from our true identity as beloved ones. We have an identity crisis and often lose a sense of our dignity. Failing to embrace Baptism and our holy origins, we may be tempted to look to artificial or cheap substitutes to bring us dignity and meaning. Our origin is in God and our greatest end in God. The Church recalls what Jesus says: "I am the Alpha and the Omega" (Rv 1:8, 22:13). Jesus is our beginning and our end.

God joins himself to the Eucharist in order to feed and strengthen us daily. We pray in the Our Father: "Give us this day our daily bread." That daily bread is not just temporal sustenance; it's miraculous! Jesus is miraculously joined to the bread and wine through the prayers of consecration at Mass. It's a total miracle. And when we consume the host and sip from the chalice, Jesus enters into us in a very simple yet profound and miraculous way. That's why the Church has long called the Eucharist *the True Presence.* Jesus is truly present in that holy food. God has joined himself together with that sacrament, and what God has joined, we must not divide.

When we separate that knowledge, or that truth, from the Eucharist, we are not receiving the Lord in faith. The Eucharist, in that case, runs the risk of becoming degraded or of little worth in our minds and hearts. In fact, the complete opposite is the truth! Jesus joins himself to us via the Eucharist again and again.

We find God's life alive in us through the sacraments. The Church invites our full confidence in God's profound presence with us through the graces we receive sacramentally.

THE BATTLE FOR THE RENEWAL OF OUR MINDS

Trusting God's sacramental system within the Church can be a battle unless we renew our minds in Christ. St. Paul writes, "Do not be conformed to this world, but be transformed by the renewing of your minds, so that you may discern what is the will of God—what is good and acceptable and perfect" (Rom 12:2). We must learn to think with the mind of Christ, otherwise we may be tempted to believe lies told about the Church that come from the evil one or from human persons who think they can outsmart or outdesign the plan of the Creator of the cosmos.

We are called to have confidence in God's good plan: "God, infinitely perfect and blessed in himself, in a plan of sheer goodness freely created man to make him share in his own blessed life" (CCC, 1).

God made us to share his blessed life. Another way of saying that is that God made us to share his *divine* life. We get a foretaste of that life in the graces we receive now, but we'll ultimately experience the fullness of such a life in heaven. So we've got to prepare. And the Church is here on earth to help us get there. She is both human and divine, like Jesus. Jesus crossed the chasm—the great divide—between heaven and earth. He built a permanent bridge *in himself*, the God-man.

Jesus came that we might experience the blessed divine life that he and the Father desire for us. The Church, the Body of Christ on earth, exists for our benefit—to bring on the final, ultimate reality. That is our destiny: to share his blessed life. Christ came to share our life so we could one day share his.

Some readers may be thinking they are reading a fiction novel—that this is a cool story but that's not how it's all going to end. I understand. We are often not acquainted with this sacred mentality or sacramental worldview. But by growing in grace—by keeping close to the sacraments of the Church—we will come to a deeper belief in all that Jesus says and does. All this both/and stuff has real meaning and ramifications.

What God has joined, we must not divide.

The world has many ways of creating dividing lines in our minds, dividing our faith in God from our trust in the Church. Our faith in God and our trust in the Church need to be knitted together in our hearts like Christmas and December 25—for belief in the Incarnation is central to Christian faith.

And that brings us back to Christmas and Jesus coming into the world and taking on a human body.

Christians for two millennia have stood in awe of this beautiful true story, and with hearts rejoicing they name this Christmas mystery the "marvelous exchange." In the prayers of the Liturgy we chant, "O marvelous exchange! Man's Creator has become man, born of a virgin. We have been made sharers in the divinity of Christ who humbled himself to share our humanity."[3]

This truth is almost beyond human comprehension. The world's greatest minds throughout the ages have believed it, too, and sought to explain the why of it. St. Athanasius, a feisty fourth-century bishop of Alexandria, spent his whole life, in and out of exile, defending the Incarnation of Christ. He wrote passionately about this marvelous exchange: "For the Son of God became man so that we might become God" (*CCC*, 460).

St. Thomas Aquinas, the prolific thirteenth-century Doctor of the Church, repeated it: "The only-begotten Son of God, wanting to make us sharers in his divinity, assumed our nature, so that he, made man, might make men gods" (*CCC*, 460).

What does this marvelous exchange mean for us? It means that we have grace to become children of God. What Jesus is by nature, we can become by grace. It does not happen right away. It takes a lifetime to become a saint—the person you were born to be.

SPIRITUAL CHILDHOOD

Jesus taught that spiritual childhood is exactly the condition we need to enter his kingdom: "Truly I tell you, unless you change and become like children, you will never enter the kingdom of heaven. Whoever becomes humble like this child is the greatest in the kingdom of heaven" (Mt 18:3–4).

St. Paul tells us it is by adoption that we become children of God, thanks to the Incarnation: "But when the fullness of time had time come, God sent his Son, born of woman, born under the law, in order to redeem those who were under the law, so that we might receive adoption as children. And because you are children, God has sent the Spirit of his Son into our hearts, crying, 'Abba! Father!'" (Gal 4:4–6).

Again, think back to Christmas, and look at the Magi—esteemed wise men from the East coming before the little infant Jesus born into poverty. The Magi, men of power and influence, knelt—*knelt!*—before Jesus (see Mt 2:11). They understood that we must become little.

During his public ministry, Jesus preached: "Very truly, I tell you, no one can see the kingdom of God without being born from above" (Jn 3:3). This was the mystery another wise man, Nicodemus, faced. He was a devout Jew in search of the truth. Hearing Jesus' words, Nicodemus asked an intelligent question: "How can anyone be born after having grown old? Can one enter a second time into the mother's womb and be born?" Jesus explained that this is possible only by "water and Spirit" (Jn 3:4–5). Does that sound familiar?

Our lives are meant to resemble this spiritual childhood. We've got to let ourselves become little in the way that Jesus did. If he entered into humility by becoming a child, so can we, even if we are grown-ups, by the power of his grace.

I learn two things from Jesus' coming as a child. The first is, from Jesus' standpoint, that childhood is a good and happy thing. The second is that the childhood of Jesus makes God approachable for us. It is no surprise why we cherish Christmas—God's nearness to us beckons us to draw close. Jesus is called Emmanuel, "God is with us" (Mt 1:23).

For many of us, childhood was a time of innocence. We went about our days without any worries, often living in the bliss of the moment. It was a very Eden-like existence up to a point. Eventually we had to grow up, to be responsible and mature and productive. There is nothing really wrong with that, except that as adults we often forget the gifts of our childhood.

Even worse, some people's memories of childhood are marred beyond recognition—stolen from them by violence or depravity. In such cases, the beauty and bliss of that child-identity—our original core connection of being a child of God—can be disjointed, disconnected, or dismembered.

Enter the Christ Child—and the dawn of something mysteriously new.

Enter the Child who stepped into time to promise eternity.

Enter the Child with the power to make children of us all.

Jesus' coming restores to us what was lost and offers a life in relationship with God. He shows us the way and invites us to follow him.

If God became a little child—slipping into the bliss of being held in the arms of his loving parents—just what does that show us? There is something holy—and necessary—about being a child. We learn to whom we belong, and we begin to know peace.

I weep at the miracle and majesty of Christmas captured in the holy Babe. I long to let go of my adult cares and slip into the bliss of being held in the folds of Jesus' robe. When I enter that mystery of Christmas, I rejoin, reconnect, and remember to whom I belong. I remember I am still a child of God regardless of my age or circumstance. I relearn to sleep, as the hymn sings, in heavenly peace.

When I kneel before the crèche, I experience the marvelous exchange that comes from baby Jesus gazing up at me.

God's plan for the world, and God's plan for me, is one I can trust and believe in.

Long ago, on that first Christmas night, Jesus, too, entered all in with utter confidence in the Father's plan.

PRAY

Meditate on the lyrics of a Christmas carol. Open a hymnal, or find the lyrics to the songs online (such as at Hymnary. org). These carols capture God's plan for us in song:

> "Hark! The Herald Angels Sing"
> "Let All Mortal Flesh Keep Silence"
> "O Little Town of Bethlehem"
> "Once in Royal David's City"
> "Silent Night"

Learn

Try to memorize the first sentence of the first paragraph of the *Catechism of the Catholic Church*: "God, infinitely perfect and blessed in himself, in a plan of sheer goodness freely created man to make him share in his own blessed life" (*CCC*, 1). If you're really ambitious, memorize the whole paragraph!

Engage

Choose one of these activities:

- Listen to the song "My Grown-Up Christmas List," recorded in recent years by both Natalie Cole and Amy Grant. (Search for the video online at YouTube.) Then write out your own grown-up Christmas list, and turn it into a prayer of petition this week by lighting a candle in a church or shrine in remembrance of those needs.
- Set up a small Christmas shrine in your home, even if this is not the right season for it. Set up small figures of the Holy Family from a Nativity set, or just set up a photo of Jesus in the manger. Put it somewhere to remind you that the message of Christmas is for every day of the year.

CHAPTER 4

The Fatherhood of God

Beloved Sons and Daughters in a Royal Family

Like many people baptized as infants, I have no memory of that special day, yet it changed my life and put me on a trajectory toward heaven. There's a photo and a baptismal certificate as proof. My parents and godparents recall it, and God most surely does, too. Yet my heart must ponder carefully the magnitude of that day. Unless you were an older child or an adult when you were baptized, you too might need to spend some time reflecting on the meaning of your baptism.

For me, it is more meaningful to recall the reality of my own baptism as I experience someone else's. I recalled my joys as each of my three children were baptized. Baptism offers the greatest gift we could bring to our children's lives—to bring them to God, to invite God's presence to live in them so that one day they might know their Father in heaven.

My baptism as an infant removed the sin I never could—original sin. After that, I was ushered into a relationship with God. I was not aware of that relationship at first. It was God's gift to me through Jesus Christ who died for me. God used the Church and my parents to bring me God's gift: God claiming me as his daughter, his child. I was a new creation that day.

Just as Jesus, the Son of God, entered our human life as an infant child, we enter the divine life we are destined for—as a child of God—when we are baptized. Our baptisms make us sons and daughters of God. Just as the Christ Child grew up to bear witness to being the Son of the Father in heaven, so must we. What Jesus models, we must follow.

Baptism makes us part of God's family. That's not a platitude; it's reality. We have supernatural ties to God—we *belong*! Again, this is part of God's plan of sheer goodness. The Trinity longs to make us beloved, alongside Jesus—to make us part of its family.

Union with God is our ultimate destiny, and Baptism is our start. In Baptism we are connected to the Holy Trinity: we become sons and daughters of the Father, coheirs with Jesus the Son, and temples of the Holy Spirit—that is, the Spirit of God dwells in us. The Catholic Church teaches that what Jesus experiences by nature, we will one day experience by grace.

The baptism of Jesus in the Jordan River reveals the Trinity. Read scripture carefully, and you'll find all the members of the Trinity in a starring role in this scene from Matthew's gospel: "And when Jesus had been baptized, just as he came up from the water, suddenly the heavens were opened to him and he saw the Spirit of God descending like a dove and alighting on him. And a voice from heaven said, 'This is my Son, the Beloved, with whom I am well pleased'" (Mt 3:16–17). Jesus comes up from the water, and the heavens open. The Spirit is present as a dove, and the Father's voice is heard. The Father speaks and even seems to gush over this Son with his words. Jesus is the

Beloved—the Father declares it! The Father acknowledges his love for the Beloved Son.

This is no brief Hallmark-greeting-card moment. No. Much more is being conveyed. If this were a movie, we would cue the dramatic music and sound effects and imagine the biggest, strongest, most commanding yet compassionate voice you've ever heard saying, "This is my Son, the Beloved, with whom I am well pleased."

Never before in the history of the universe had the voice of God been heard like this. This utterance comes from the immortal, omnipotent, omnipresent, omniscient, heavenly Creator. The Eternal Father pours more love than the cosmos can hold into the perfect Beloved Son, who blesses all the waters of the earth as he immerses himself—and who rises again in the waters of baptism.

This is a powerful moment. The Father's love is limitless and constantly poured into his Son, the Son for whom the star of Bethlehem was hung and the choirs of angels sang. Now the Father is pleased to introduce Jesus *personally* at the start of his public ministry on earth.

This is same voice of the Creator, our Father God. It is the same voice that speaks a word and—*bang!*—the universe, and the world as we know it, is brought into existence, made from nothing. God's voice also pours out creative, life-giving love, designing human beings in his image. The book of Genesis recounts the interior conversation of the Three-in-One: "Let us make humankind in our image" (Gn 1:26).

At Jesus' baptism the Holy Spirit's power and presence is carefully under wraps, represented by a dove. In reality, the Spirit is anything but small. That dove is the same majestic and mighty Spirit of God that hovered over the waters when the heavens and the earth first began (see Gn 1:1–2).

Let's imagine our own baptisms as we consider this biblical drama. We see the water used in Baptism—a gift of creation—and we are immersed in it, as Jesus was. Then we hear the word—the voice—of God claiming us as his own. The prayers and the Rite of Baptism spoken by the priest or deacon's voice, together with the water, make us God's children. God Almighty's voice, veiled as a human voice, utters and invokes our baptisms in the name of the Father, the Son, and the Holy Spirit. The same Holy Spirit is also present in power and majesty as the water and anointing take place at Baptism.

Almighty God is crazy in love with us. Baptism is the great eternal sign of that love! Baptism is a free gift—another reason why belonging to the Church matters!

Just as Jesus is the Beloved Son of God, Baptism allows us to share in the belovedness of the Son. God chose to love us first by making us in his image. Then he sent his Beloved Son, Jesus, to show us what real love and real life looks like, so we could know our belovedness and our redemption, both now, and, one day, in heaven.

At his ascension into heaven, Jesus' parting instructions to the Church were to "make disciples . . . baptizing them in the name of the Father and of the Son and of the Holy Spirit" (Mt 28:19). The Church has never wavered in following those instructions, even to the present day. The Church baptizes because Jesus commands it, that we might know the God who loves us.

Baptism takes place only once, but the graces of Baptism have ripple effects—building a foundation for a life of love, a life of resembling the Beloved.

Our first birth is our birthday. However, Baptism is a new or second birth, a re-creation of who we are in Christ. It is a spiritual rebirth.

We are not just born into a nuclear family, but into *God's family*. And in God's family, all of the siblings share the same godly DNA. We are all reborn, in a real sense, to resemble our brother, Jesus. We are to imitate Jesus, to walk and talk and think and love like he does. It's a life-long transformation that God accomplishes in us through grace if we let him. The very first graces we get come from Baptism.

In the earliest days of the Church, believers were usually baptized as adults. A person made an intentional, conscious decision to be *for* Christ. A candidate for Baptism would turn away from bad stuff (sin, vice, evil, the devil) and turn toward God's love by asking for Baptism. It was a long process, called the *catechumenate*, or preparation time. (Today, we see that preparation time for adults in the Rite of Christian Initiation for Adults.)

Many of us baptized as infants or children may wonder why we weren't given the chance or the freedom to choose Baptism. Why not wait until we could choose Christ for ourselves?

I've learned to be at peace with those questions. For me, belonging to the Church set the stage for the moment—when I *knew* Jesus was with me on the bench that day—when I chose Jesus for myself with a young adult's heart. The graces of Baptism were already priming the pump, so to speak, preparing the way for God to use a kind of catechumenate process in my own life. I can trace it sparking into flame in the years following my Confirmation. And trust me, decades later I'm still a work in progress. Yet today I'm more confident of God's plan for me and his abundant love for me. His timing for things to unfold for me is best.

With infant Baptism, the Church operates like a mother trying to save her children from harm. That's why infant Baptism quickly became a standard practice in the Early Church. Baptism is given only with the full consent of the parents of the child. Parents make the decision, with support of godparents, not to delay Baptism because its effects are so wonderful and powerful!

Here's why the Church offers parents infant or child Baptism. Each child is born into a broken and fallen world.

What's worse, each human person inherits original sin, a separation from God that cannot be overcome on one's own. It's true. We need grace, and we cannot manufacture God's merciful love on our own. It's a total and free gift that comes from Jesus' death and resurrection. His Cross gained our salvation. God's mercy and gratuitous love bridge the gap between us. And God freely wants to do this for us out of love for us.

There is danger in staying separated from God over the course of time. It makes one susceptible to the ways of darkness and the devil. Baptism transforms all of that.

In Baptism, God welcomes the child as his own, and the presence of God, the Holy Spirit, fills the child. The famous part of Baptism, the pouring on of holy water or immersion into that water, is where Baptism obliterates original sin. It brings God's light into darkness and immediately makes the newly baptized a child of God.

Among other important signs and prayers in the Rite of Baptism, the person's name is spoken together with the threefold name of God, in the Trinitarian formula that we know from the Sign of the Cross. Think again of how the Holy Trinity showed up at Jesus' baptism. The Holy Trinity is present at every baptism, as evidenced when the priest or deacon pronounces these words: "I baptize you, N., in the name of the Father, and of the Son, and of the Holy Spirit."

This baptized person is now a son or daughter of God, with whom he is well pleased. That moment forms a permanent bond between the Triune God—the Father, the Son, and the Holy Spirit—and that person.

The anointing with oil at Baptism imparts a sacred seal, or what the Church calls a sacred "character," that marks the beloved one's soul. It's an invisible sign to us, but it is seen by God as a holy brand of belonging to his family. It's like receiving a signet ring or a coat of arms or family crest that identifies the beloved child as royalty, belonging to a kingly family. I've often likened it to a soul tattoo. God makes us his own—not as property but as treasured princes or princesses of the divine King.

When an infant or very young child is baptized, the Church presumes that the child's catechumenate, or spiritual training, will take place later in life. At their child's baptism, parents make promises to provide this training. (You can read all about the Rite of Baptism—each of the steps, the promises, profession of faith, and the blessings— in the document listed in the endnotes.[1])

Those of us baptized as infants need others to hand on its significance to us. We need to be raised and nurtured in the faith. We need to understand the value of our baptisms and to choose for ourselves to live according to its promises. In some families and churches, this is a sacred trust passed down to children with great love and devotion. Not so for others.

For those who are lacking this training, do not give up hope. There are many great saints in heaven who did not start their training for holiness until later in life. We all have to start somewhere. Just know that if you are baptized, you have a great foundation to build on. And if you are not baptized, you might wish to inquire about it.

An Ever-Present, Almighty Father and a Spiritual Family

Let's consider what it means to have God as our heavenly Father.

As members of the family of God, we have a larger family beyond our family of origin. Beyond the goodness or perhaps beyond the heartaches that we may have experienced in our earthly families of origin, God has a place for us. Our name and our existence are precious to him!

God will never disown us or divorce us. We may choose to leave him, but he will never leave us! And even if we've managed to get lost or walk away, he is forever a forgiving Father awaiting our return. That seal on our soul is always visible to him. He has chosen and claimed us as his own. We belong to him forever. Yet we must choose to return his love.

The Father Almighty, as we address him in the Creed, is truly bigger than the fears, tears, and jeers that we may suffer in our earthly relationships. God the Father is the source of all grace and the epitome of a listening parent who longs to scoop us up and console us. God the Father never abandons us. He never forgets us. He never checks out. He is present 24/7.

How can we trust this to be true? Because Jesus is trustworthy. During his years on earth, Jesus pointed to the Father and revealed his ever-present nearness in many ways.

Jesus gave us the words to the Our Father (see Mt 6:9–13). He preached about the love of fathers in parables (see Lk 15:11–32; Mt 21:28–31), and he modeled his own relationship with the Father by pausing and going off alone to be with the Father in prayer (see Mk 1:35; Mt 6:9–13, 11:24–26, 14:23; Lk 6:12, 22:41–44).

Echoing the example of her Bridegroom, Jesus, the Church prays to the Father in her worship. At Mass, and at other moments, the Church gathers to pray as one to God our Father.

The Church is a supernatural family of God while at the same time being made up of human persons and human frailties. Yet the graces present in that Church have helped her to thrive for millennia.

The idea of having a supernatural family in God offers me hope when I'm doubting or hurting with regard to family. Having a Father in heaven brings me peace when I struggle in my own family here on earth.

The hurts we may suffer in our families, especially with regard to fatherhood, may obscure the goodness and greatness of knowing our Father in heaven—a reliable

Father, one who is worthy of our trust. In my younger years, I had communication struggles with my earthly father, and he with me. We both yelled a lot, and it got pretty heated at times. It often led to hurt feelings and a silent brooding on my part. Yet here's the simple truth of my baptism in all of this: I learned that just because my earthly dad and I were sometimes on the outs, it did not mean that God and I were. Father God's heart was still open to me. Similiarly, as I faced my own struggles as a parent in later years and messed things up with my own kids, I could still turn to my loving Father in heaven for love, support, and guidance.

Over the years, knowledge of my heavenly Father has helped to soothe the aches suffered in my earthly families and also provided me strength and help to improve the situations that were troublesome. It's not easy to love others without making mistakes. Yet my baptism assures me of my relationship with a heavenly parent. Through prayer and the sacraments, I have found healing for the wounds I suffer here in my earthly relationships, and I receive forgiveness and reconciliation for my errors. God the Father, in a sense, has reparented me where I've failed or where I've suffered hurts.

Baptism assures me that God the Father desires union with me in this life and in the next. Through the Church he has provided the graces I need to grow into that union more and more—both in my earthly family and within his family.

Talking, Listening, Confessing, Forgiving

By learning to pray and staying close to the sacraments—by remaining in the family God—I have access to the benefits of the Church's wisdom and graces for everyday life.

Prayer connects me to my heavenly parent, a doting and devoted Father to whom I can turn to any hour of the day or night. Prayer is the strongest wireless connection we can have!

There's no static with God the Father—prayer can communicate all of our longings and struggles and even our victories! Through prayer—talking to God and listening to God—both in my private daily prayers and in my communal prayers with the Church, I have received countless graces in order to love others better. I've learned to be less selfish and to rejoice in being a member of a family, warts and all.

Baptism paves the way for the graces that will flow from confession and the sacrament of Reconciliation as well as the Eucharist. I'll be talking about the Eucharist a bit later, but for now, let me sing the praises of going to confession—and its benefits for me and the family of God.

The sacrament of Reconciliation affirms my life as a daughter of God. When my princess tiara gets a little askew, or, ahem, I'm really not living up to my Christian dignity as a baptized child of God, I go to confession and get things right between God and me. After I do so, I am unburdened and feel much lighter. After Reconciliation, I possess the resolve to live a life of love with greater zeal.

Holding on to sin means we have too much to carry. Our hands and our hearts are too encumbered to receive all the gifts that God our Father wants to lavish on us, given the dignity we have in our birthright, Baptism.

A few years back, while I was making my annual retreat, I went to confession. I wanted to clean the slate between God and myself. And I received a lot more than anticipated.

In confession I unexpectedly released a deep emotional hurt and years of resentment toward someone. I had not planned on confessing that. In fact, as I prepared for my turn in the confessional, it was not even on my mind. There were other things to confess! Yet somehow in the course of my conversation with the priest, it was as if a dam opened up and this old hurt surfaced in my mind, and the Holy Spirit prompted me and pointed to *that! Mention that!*

I did, and that smelly, ancient history was gone. It was lifted right out of me. It was a tender, grace-filled moment with Jesus in the person of the priest. I made an Act of Contrition, and I was forgiven and absolved of my sin and resentment.

Minutes later in the pew, clutching a few tissues after my prayers of penance, I lingered in the peaceful presence of God. I was on retreat, after all, and I even had a new Bible next to me on the pew bench. I had bought it to go on retreat and was using it for the first time.

I opened my Bible to the fifth chapter of John. The words on the sacred page seemed as if they were written just for me. The text described Jesus' instantaneous healing of a paralyzed man whose affliction had disabled him for thirty-eight years. In that moment, I knew the formerly paralyzed person mentioned in the Bible was me. I had just experienced something lifted from my heart that had crippled me for the same amount of time: thirty-eight years. *Whoa.*

Those verses were a second gift from Jesus, a bonus added to the graces already given to me, no doubt, so I wouldn't miss the point. Jesus could not have been any more real to me than if he walked into the chapel and sat down next to me. That confession and its aftermath stayed with me for some time. I've come to cherish that healing. And when I'm tempted to resume being paralyzed by that old resentment, I recall that, in Christ, it no longer has a power over me.

That moment in the chapel was another in a series of *Jesus moments* in my life. I could never have constructed it or imagined it on my own. It was totally orchestrated by him. Like a lover's spontaneous kiss that renders me speechless, it begs only to be received. It was like the mountaintop, like the bench, like oh-so-many moments when his love breaks through to me.

That night Jesus was present to me in both moments: in the sacrament that was a holy intervention of his grace and in his living word to me afterward. Through reconciliation, the dignity of my baptism spoke to me, too. I was a beloved daughter, and my Father was well pleased that I was coming to him with my need.

Thanks to the guidance of my heavenly Father and his Son, Jesus Christ, I've experienced positive changes and intergenerational healings in my relationships—with my earthly parents and with my own children—over the course of time.

We derive benefits from being called children of God, most especially when we ask for the graces to live according to that identity.

HOME WITH THE FATHER, HEIRS WITH CHRIST

Baptism shows us that God desires union *with* us. So I'm equally moved by Jesus' words that illustrate God's desire to make his *home in* us: "Those who love me will keep my word, and my Father will love them, and we will come to them and make our home with them" (Jn 14:23).

God wants to have a home in us, in me and in you. When I accept this, I too live as if I am at home with God and in God. Having a home with God helps me stay grounded. I can feel at home even when life at my family home seems difficult.

Knowing I have a home in God renews me. It refreshes me and helps to send me back to my family, job, community, or church prepared to do better—to try again to love and to forgive all things as far as possible, again and again. By doing that—by allowing God to make his home in us now—we become the means for his love to work through us and to be made manifest in the world.

Ultimately, belonging to both my earthly family and my family of God in the Church is a cure for selfishness. It's a training ground for holiness. Family life is designed to lead us toward God's best for us. Holiness is a movement toward heaven and permanent union with God. Through our baptisms, God takes up residence in us on earth so we can learn to live one day in our heavenly home.

The sooner we live with God in peace—following his word and ways—the better we can understand his making a home in us. We won't always do this well, but Jesus teaches us to focus on our coming home to the Father and to see our Father as benevolent, one who has our best interests at heart.

Jesus' parable of the prodigal son, also known as the parable of the forgiving father, gives us a true image of the fatherhood of God (see Lk 15:11–32). Both the returning prodigal son and the resentful older brother viewed their father in limited ways. They perceived him through the lens of their youthful experiences and their birth order. They did not yet see their father in his fullness—his magnanimity, his generosity, or his ardent and transforming love. Instead, it seems to me, they mistook him as his authority, his wealth, and his work. Toward the end of the parable, we see that both of his sons were mistaken about their father's heart, his intentions, and the depth of his love for each of them. The father clearly embraces both—through the welcome party and filial gifts given to the younger son and through the equally significant pledge that "all that is mine is yours" (Lk 15:31) to the elder son.

How often have we been mistaken about God our Father? Do we too see only his holy authority, missing out on his loving fatherliness? I know I have suffered because of that but only when I did not have a strong sense of my birthright, my baptism, and my belonging.

Our baptism makes us not only children of God, but heirs of God with Christ! "For all who are led by the Spirit of God are children of God. For you did not receive a spirit of slavery to fall back into fear, but you have received the spirit of adoption. When we cry, 'Abba! Father!' it is that very Spirit bearing witness with our spirit that we are children of God, and if children, then heirs, heirs of God and joint heirs with Christ—if, in fact, we suffer with him so that we may also be glorified with him" (Rom 8:14–17). Proper heirs receive a portion of their father's estate. The disposal of property to the rightful heirs has always been the kingdom plan. If God is our Father then Jesus is our brother. If God the Father reigns over the kingdom then Jesus is heir to all the kingdom has to offer, just as any Son would be.

The kingdom of God is our inheritance. We, then, must act like heirs. Think of it in terms of bloodline. Jesus' Incarnation—his taking on flesh and blood—makes him one of us. He is our brother who, by his dying and rising, brings us back to the Father. Our baptisms point to this truth. We are heirs with Christ. By the power of his blood, we possess a new lineage. "It is as if, by bestowing his grace on us in the sacraments, God gives us a divine blood transfusion, his eternal life being poured into our souls, enabling and preparing us to be united with him."[2]

Christian faith invites us to imitate Jesus, the first-born Son and our brother. In Baptism, we are marked by the *Sign of the Cross*. There is no escaping this. We may indeed suffer, but Baptism and the other sacraments that follow release such powerful graces that even those of us in the toughest circumstances can endure and still continue to grow spiritually. Our inheritance, even if we have to suffer with Christ, will be to reign with him.

Baptism is not only about becoming the beloved children of God; it's about becoming more conformed to Christ, the Beloved. We are called to live a life of service and goodness *in imitation of Jesus*. This is so that, one day, each beloved child of God will be able to reign in heaven with the Beloved Son, our brother.

Heaven is our destiny. It will be our inheritance if we trust our truest identity and remember what Baptism promises us—new life! This very day, we may be being prepared for eternity. The Church acts as a nurturing mother to prepare her children for this heavenly home.

I'm beloved of God, thanks to my baptism. My identity, and the true depths of who I am, comes from this familial relationship with God. Baptism makes me a beloved daughter of God the Father. My elder brother Jesus afforded this to me through his life, death, and resurrection. And the Holy Spirit empowers me to live it like I mean it. Becoming a disciple of Jesus means accepting the invitation to belong to *God's family*, to live in conformity with his way of life: "For whoever does the will of my Father in heaven is my brother, and sister, and mother [Mt 12:49]" (*CCC*, 2233).

I thank God for the Church who baptizes, as instructed by Jesus, in the name of the Father, the Son, and the Holy Spirit. Even though I have no memory of the day of my baptism, the Holy Trinity remembers me every day and awaits my homecoming! In the meantime, I'm making lifelong memories of my own within the family of God!

PRAY

St. Hilary of Poitiers taught, "Everything that happened to Christ lets us know that, after the bath of water, the Holy Spirit swoops down upon us from high heaven and that, adopted by the Father's voice, we become sons of God" (*CCC*, 537). Besides at Jesus' baptism, there is another event, as recorded by three gospels, where the Father's voice is heard.

Meditate on the Transfiguration of Jesus. Find it in Matthew 17:1–8, Mark 9:2–8, and Luke 9:28–36.

LEARN

Read about the fatherhood of God in the *Catechism of the Catholic Church*, paragraphs 232–235, 270, and 272.

Read about Baptism in the *Catechism*. There is a large, comprehensive section devoted to Baptism in paragraphs 1213–1284. If time is short, skip to these suggested paragraphs: 537, 1213–1216, 1224, 1226–1227, 1253–1255, 1257, and 1262–1272.

ENGAGE

Celebrate your baptism! If you don't already know it, find out the date that you were baptized. Then add it to your permanent calendar. Just as you might celebrate your birthday, find an appropriate way to celebrate your baptismal day. In my family, we had a special plate that rotated among family members' special days at dinner, including baptismal days, and we always added a fun dessert after the meal. In addition, I attend Mass, in thanksgiving, on my baptismal day, and I telephone my parents, who brought me to baptism. Someday I hope to revisit the church where I was baptized.

If you haven't been baptized, you can explore the opportunity by visiting a Roman Catholic Church and scheduling time to speak with a priest.

CHAPTER 5

THE MOTHERHOOD OF THE CHURCH

CONFIDENCE IN MARY AS MOTHER

I was nineteen years old and yelling and chanting at the top of my lungs in a packed house at Madison Square Garden: "J-P-2! We-love-you! J-P-2! We-love-you!" The pope smiled and leaned into the microphone, saying, "I love you, too!" In 1979, before there was such a thing as World Youth Day, I took my youth group to see Pope John Paul II at a youth rally. He electrified the audience, and his message was "Look to Christ who gives you the meaning of life." As I grew older, I paid attention to the inspired things Pope John Paul II said and did. He was pope for twenty-seven years of my life. I found that he never stopped pointing out the meaning of life.

John Paul II's pontificate woke me up to Mary. And in many ways, the now-saint woke me up to the motherhood of the Church.

Pope John Paul II's motto was *Totus Tuus*, or "totally yours." This described his personal entrustment of his life to Jesus through Mary as his mother and teacher. John Paul II was one of the smartest men of his age, an intellectual giant: a philosopher, theologian, playwright, author, poet, and polyglot. Yet in his young life and throughout his priesthood and papacy, he was unabashedly devoted to the Blessed Virgin Mary.

John Paul II was shot in St. Peter's Square on May 13, 1981. Wounded by close-range bullets in the assassination attempt, he attributed his escape from death to Mary. John Paul II later commented that while one hand pulled the trigger, "a motherly hand" guided the bullets. Did the would-be assassin know that he happened to carry out his plot on the feast day devoted to Our Lady of Fatima—a beloved spiritual mother of John Paul II? I guess not. John Paul II was one of Mary's devoted sons.

When he recovered physically from the attack, the grateful pope presented a bullet to the bishop of Leira-Fátima as a gift for the shrine of Our Lady of Fatima in Portugal. The bishop promptly had jewelers set the bullet into the ornate crown that adorns Mary's statue there. A lethal slug is now forever transformed into a beautiful sign of maternal protection and a son's humble gratitude.

In my first book, *Blessed, Beautiful, and Bodacious*,[1] I unpacked the dignity, gifts, and mission of women—what St. John Paul II dubbed "the feminine genius." In that book I also described my ongoing relationship with Mary, the Blessed Mother.

Between my late twenties and thirties, there was a progressive movement in my affections for Mary. I went from knowing about Mary to getting to know her as my mother. It was a slow process—let's call it "making friends"—bringing Mary more deeply into my confidence. The trajectory moved from my knowing Mary as an acquaintance to more of a friend to ultimately discovering a filial connection in my heart.

Praying the Rosary and praying with the gospels about Mary's life of faith opened my heart. I began with knowing Mary as a historical and biblical figure and then moved on to knowing her as the mother of Jesus. As I began to consider her life, I started envisioning her as a woman of prayer and great courage. As I pondered Mary's relationship with Jesus, I began to know her as a trustworthy guide, friend, and prayer partner.

Mary became my prayer buddy—and *geez*, did I need her help at the time! I was a young mom struggling with feelings of failure and frustration in mothering my young family. I fell short of patience and charity and was long on anger and fatigue. Too many things provoked harsh responses in me. I was not being fair to my husband or children. I needed some big-time motherhood coaching and, frankly, some inner healing that I did want to admit I needed regarding anger.

One day in my prayer, as I pondered Jesus' passion and death on the Cross, I read these words from John's gospel with new eyes: "When Jesus saw his mother and the disciple whom he loved standing beside her, he said to his mother, 'Woman, here is your son.' Then he said to the disciple, 'Here is your mother.' And from that hour the disciple took her into his own home" (Jn 19:26–27).

That last simple phrase about the beloved disciple caught me off guard—*the disciple took her into his own home.* I too wished to be a beloved disciple like John. Yet so often in my life, I had only been giving Mary lip service. I often treated Mary as some kind of fairy godmother who just floated around waiting to answer my prayers or solve my problems. Of course a good mother wants to help her children solve problems. Yet all along I think Mary knew I had to mature in my love for her and my love for Jesus. I asked them both to help me be a better mother, for that's where I struggled and failed the most.

I soon learned that there was a direct correlation between who I was on the inside and what I did on the outside. The deeper I went with Jesus, with Mary's help and inspiration, the more meaningful my motherhood became and the better my parenting.

Eventually I realized Mary was truly a gift for my growth in becoming a better person. She was mothering me along—and it was all Jesus' idea in the first place! Jesus confirmed this reality for me in that scene at Calvary. Mary's spiritual motherhood was Jesus' final gift from the Cross.

The Church teaches that when Jesus speaks to the beloved disciple, John—"Here is your mother" (Jn 19:27)—he is speaking to *all* beloved disciples, both in the present and future tense, for all time.

Prior to those hands-on mothering years, I had largely ignored Mary and most certainly never invited Mary to make her home in my home. Things were too messy there to invite in the Mother of God!

My prayers back then were like a transaction: *I will say these Rosaries in hopes of something good happening.* Today I'd call that a "gumball machine" spirituality: *I'll put my quarter into the slot and see what candy pops out.* I'm not criticizing faithful, humble petitioning here. I still pray and ask for things all the time! God desires those prayers of petition from us. But I'm disappointed by how often I made the mistake of falling in love with the *gifts* I received and not the *giver* of the gifts.

God calls us to pray, to have an ongoing relationship with him—and with all his saints. But I often reduced prayers of petition to a selfish case of *the gimmes*, being preoccupied with what it was going to get me.

My desperate need to be a more nurturing and gracious mother meant I was willing to try anything to succeed, so I gave Mary a chance.

To give a home to Mary—to allow her to move into my life—was the beginning of a new kind of discipleship training for me. It was a way to become a better follower of Christ. This was getting personal. This was allowing Mary to coach me, to mentor me, to allow her good influence to find a home in me.

Mary's openness to God allowed God to do good work through her. She allowed her will to be aligned with his. She modeled that for me and challenged me to try it. Mary became much more than a prayer buddy. She mothered me, helping me simmer down in my restlessness and frustrations on many fronts, but especially in my parenting. She helped me count the blessings and joys amid my many struggles and screwups.

I wasn't just a sinner—I was a *loved* sinner.

SAY YES, THEN DO WHATEVER HE TELLS YOU

As I prayed the Rosary with more fervor and meditated on its Mysteries (the truths captured in the Rosary), it took on new potency. I began to understand the significance of the annunciation—another monumental moment in the history of the universe—when the Incarnation took place! Jesus took flesh in Mary's womb, thanks to her loving consent and generous cooperation with God's divine plan: "Then Mary said, 'Here am I, the servant of the Lord; let it be with me according to your word'" (Lk 1:38). (Read the whole thing! See Lk 1:26–38.) "The Annunciation to Mary was the unique moment when God placed the whole weight of human history in the hands of one person."[2] Mary was all in for God in the greatest of ways.

When Mary offered her *fiat*, her *let-it-be*, to the heavenly Father to become the mother of God's Son, she set into motion an event more incredible than the Big Bang. St. John Paul II, using the beloved disciple's texts, reflects on it as "the moment fixed from all eternity when the Father sent his Son 'that whoever believes in him should not perish but have eternal life' (Jn 3:16) . . . the blessed moment when the Word that 'was with God . . . became flesh and dwelt among us' (Jn 1:1, 14)."[3]

Mary's fiat had ramifications not only for her own life but also for all future followers of Jesus. Her yes shows us that living for God is saying yes to God and welcoming him in! Mary was the first true disciple of Jesus.

Through Mary my youthful teenaged love of Jesus was reignited and brought to maturity. I learned to love God with a rekindled passion—as a woman learning to love for all she is worth and capable of making sacrifices for the sake of love. Mary taught me what it meant to be a person of prayer and of action. She offered confident advice for keeping my eyes trained on Jesus: "Do whatever he tells you" (Jn 2:5).

Slowly, I changed for the better. Mary helped me fall deeper in love with Jesus, my husband, and my children as I served them. It was a spiritual makeover by grace. I had greater peace and deeper joy—all because I asked Mary into my home, taking her as my spiritual mother.

Momma Mary loves you, too. You can be confident that she gives the best help to her children. She loves it when we say yes to loving her son, Jesus. But she's even more overjoyed when we do whatever he tells us to do.

MARY'S LINK TO THE MOTHERHOOD OF THE CHURCH

As I became more confident in my faith, I was eager to share it with my family and friends. Yet I needed to know more about the Catholic faith myself! Mary's gentle words, "Do whatever he tells you," made me pay more attention to Catholic things. I felt called to better understand the Church's teachings. Ensconced in my stay-at-home mothering, I drank in the nurture of the Church's motherhood. I read all I could about the Church's wisdom. I read so much that I eventually enrolled in graduate school for theology.

Something I learned along the way is that Mary's motherhood and the Church's motherhood bear similarities that we cannot ignore. We'll get to the motherhood of the Church shortly, but first let's stay on Mary.

Mary's motherhood of Jesus means that she is inextricably linked to all of his followers, the Body of Christ, the Church. St. Pius X taught that this important reality began with that very first yes, Mary's fiat.

> For is not Mary the Mother of Christ? Then she is our Mother also. . . .
>
> Wherefore in . . . his most chaste Mother Christ took to Himself flesh, and united to Himself the spiritual body formed by those who were to believe in Him. Hence *Mary, carrying the Savior within her, may be said to have also carried all those whose life was contained in the life of the Savior. Therefore all we who are united to Christ, and as the Apostle says are members of His body, of His flesh, and of His bones (Eph 5:30), have issued from the womb of Mary like a body united to its head. Hence, though in a spiritual and mystical fashion, we are all children of Mary, and she is Mother of us all.* Mother, spiritually indeed, but truly Mother of the members of Christ.[4]

You just might want to read that paragraph from St. Pius X again. It's fantastic.

After the annunciation, as Mary carried Jesus in her womb, she was also carrying, in a spiritual way, all those whom Jesus would one day save and who would become one with his Body.

In a certain sense, *we* who are the Body of Christ were also carried in Mary's womb! Trying to grasp this, I can think of only one analogy (and in the words a former professor of mine, "all analogies limp"). In a way, it reminds me of my own pregnancies. As I carried a child in my womb, I was also carrying, in a certain sense, my future grandchildren! It's an imperfect analogy, especially

so because God has no grandchildren! God only has sons
and daughters!

Both Vatican II and the *Catechism of the Catholic Church*
proclaim that Mary is our mother "in the order of grace"
(*CCC*, 968). Mary is our spiritual mother because of her
faithful surrender to and unity with the Father's will. Her
motherhood of us comes, first, by her agreeing to become
the Mother of God at the time of the annunciation and,
second, by her sharing in the life and work of Jesus, especially his passion and death. Mary is now our mother in
heaven, and there is no end to her mothering. She is our
mother forever.

I appreciate Pope Benedict XVI's preaching on this:
"These privileges were not granted in order to distance
Mary from us but, on the contrary, to bring her close;
indeed, since she was totally with God, this woman is very
close to us and helps us as a mother. . . . The unique and
unrepeatable position that Mary occupies . . . stems from
her fundamental vocation [as] Mother of the Redeemer.
Precisely as such, Mary is also Mother of the Mystical Body
of Christ, which is the Church."[5] From the moment Mary
was a mother, she was mother to Jesus and to us! We might
have ignored Mary out of rebellion or ignorance, but she
will never ignore us. She cannot. She has a motherly link to
each one who belongs to the Son. We can be certain of that.

Jesus' Incarnation created an important link between
Mary and the Church. "What was once granted in the
flesh to Mary is now granted spiritually to the Church."[6]
Mary's life prefigures the motherhood of the Church. The
maternal love we find in Mary is found also in the Church.
What God accomplished in Mary, Jesus brings about in
the Church.

CONFIDENCE IN THE CHURCH AS A MOTHER

When a Christian "speaks of the Church as his mother, he is not giving way to some sentimental impulse; he is expressing a reality."[7]

Pope Francis has a deep devotion to Mary. Yet he also speaks lovingly of the Church as a mother. He says, "The birth of Jesus from the womb of Mary, in fact, is the prelude to the rebirth of every Christian in the womb of the Church."[8]

Once again, we recognize what we have seen before: *what God has joined, we must not divide.* The Incarnation brings deep meaning to the Church and to this idea of the Church being our mother. God has linked Mary's motherhood with that of the Church, as she is the mother of the Church's founder, Jesus Christ. Thanks to the Incarnation of Jesus, God's fatherhood is made known to us in the face and life and work of Jesus.

Jesus' great love for his Bride, the Church, makes the Church a fruitful mother of many spiritual children, born through Baptism. The Church nurtures them though the Word of God and the graces of the seven sacraments. Therefore, the family of God is born of the fatherhood of God and the motherhood of the Church.

The motherhood of the Church is discovered and expressed in the words of the New Testament's familial language: in the words of Jesus and in the preaching of apostles. We see it, too, in the teaching of the Early Church Fathers and the saints.

Jesus used maternal imagery as he wept over the mistakes of the people of Jerusalem, the children of Israel. "Jerusalem, Jerusalem, the city that kills the prophets and stones those who are sent to it! How often have I desired to gather your children together as a hen gathers her brood under her wings, and you were not willing!" (Mt 23:37).

The Church as mother begs deep affection from her offspring, the children of God. The apostle Paul, more than once, spoke with familial terms about the people he preached to and served in the family of God: "My little children, for whom I am again in the pain of childbirth until Christ is formed in you" (Gal 4:19). (See also 1 Thes 2:7–8, 10–13.)

The beloved disciple, John, writes in his second epistle: "The elder to the elect lady and her children, whom I love in the truth, and not only I but also all who know the truth, because of the truth that abides in us and will be with us forever" (2 Jn 1:1–2).

St. Clement of Alexandria, from the third century, describes tender affection toward Mother Church: "'Like a mother consoles her son,' says the Lord (Is 66:13), 'I myself will also console you.' The mother draws her little children into her arms and we—we seek our mother, the Church."[9]

St. Cyprian, a third-century bishop and martyr, famously taught this easy-to-recall aphorism: "No one can have God as Father who does not have the Church as Mother" (CCC, 181).

Origen, a third-century theologian, repeated Cyprian's sentiment; "He who leaves the Church makes himself responsible for his own death. . . . He who does not have the Church as his mother cannot have God for father."[10]

These are powerful and sometimes harsh-sounding words to our modern ears. Yet the Early Church was a persecuted Church who spoke in strident ways to be clear in announcing to her audience the necessity of belonging to the Church and adhering to her teachings.

St. Augustine, a fourth-century bishop, described the baptismal font as the uterus of Mother Church. He taught, "The Church is a mother for us. . . . It is from her that we were born spiritually. No one can find a paternal welcome from God if he scorns his mother, the Church."[11]

A MOTHER DIFFERENT THAN WE MIGHT EXPECT

The Church as a mother operates both similarly and differently to mothers of human families.

The similarity of Mother Church to our human mothers is that she gives birth, via Baptism, to children of her Beloved Spouse. She longs that her children will experience the love and identity of being in God's family. The food and sustenance she provides are graces and blessings Mother Church speaks words that unite her family. She opposes division. She longs for communion with each and every child she brings to birth. She offers her teaching so her children can grow strong and wise and capable in the Christian life. She yearns that her children find the fullness of life in this world and in the next.

There are dissimilarities between Mother Church and human mothers, too. The upbringing many of us have experienced is one where grown children leave the sphere of a mother's influence. Most leave home and start homes of their own. Yet Mother Church's children not only are born in her but they are born to never leave her. They are called to stay and to find communion with one another. There her children can be fed and have the graces of the sacraments lavished upon them. If children depart from her, they depart from the spiritual food and nourishment they need. As we heard from Cyprian and Augustine, our salvation depends on our union with our mother, the Church.

In the heart of every child is the natural desire to think highly of its mother, with great affection. Yet sometimes as we grow, we can have disillusionments or disagreements with our mothers. No natural mother can love her children perfectly. All human love suffers from brokenness to some degree.

Human frailties affect our relationship with the Church. We get hurt in the natural life. Sometimes our natural relationships with the people who make up the Church are upsetting, and we let these relationships cause a split with our mother, the Church. Often when dealing with disappointments, we have seen only the human side of the Church, the human side that sins, without recalling the divine part of the Church. Yet grace's power can help us forgive *seventy times seven times!* (see Mt 18:22).

As we have matured in our natural lives, some of us have found the fortitude and the wisdom to make peace with our mothers in our families of origin, whom we may have disagreed with or been estranged from. The same needs to hold true in the spiritual life.

The divinity of Mother Church comes from her union with Jesus Christ. The part of the Church that is linked with her divine Spouse, Jesus, calls us to return home, to be open to being healed by the graces of communion.

Today many children of God have been ignoring or, worse, scorning their mother, the Church. Some behave as if they have no mother at all. They have no sense of belonging to the Body of Christ. Many of us have willfully decided to go our own way. This is why I've spent so much time talking about belonging. Belonging is a two-way street.

No matter where guilt for the breach lies, we can look to the apostles and the saints to tell us the truth: Mother Church is real and is the source for all the graces we need on this side of eternity. This does not negate or excuse the sins of those Catholics in the Church—the human side—who may have hurt or disappointed us. But grace gives us the power to forgive and offer a kinder look toward our offenders who have lost their way.

This is good advice from the late Catholic author Henri Nouwen, S.J.:

When we have been wounded by the Church, our temptation is to reject it. But when we reject the Church it becomes very hard for us to keep in touch with the living Christ. When we say, "I love Jesus, but I hate the Church," we end up losing not only the Church but Jesus too. The challenge is to forgive the Church. This challenge is especially great because the Church seldom asks us for forgiveness, at least not officially. But the Church as an often fallible human organization needs our forgiveness, while the Church as the living Christ among us continues to offer us forgiveness.[12]

We must not forsake, by our negative struggles with pride, ignorance, neglect, or unresolved hurts, what God has given us in the Catholic Church. Mother Church can supply the graces and opportunities we need to heal. Renewal of our relationship with the Church is worthy of our efforts. As in all relationships, our attempts to come together are always more blessed than stalwart separations. Communion is always better than isolation. What God has joined together, let us not separate.

The Church is a family. We must live the "we" of the Church, not stay stuck in the church of "me." Like family who share DNA and familial characteristics, we share a common Father and Mother. We have a Beloved Brother in Jesus, whose blood we share as we hold to a common creed, sacraments, and worship.

The Church as mother was part of the Father's will for us, to nurture the divine life in us. We *never* outgrow our need for our Mother Church, the *Mater Ecclesia*, until we reach heaven.

THE CHURCH IS A MOTHER AND TEACHER

Pope Francis says, "The Church is a Mother who teaches us to speak the language of faith."[13] Nurture and education are animating principles of Christian life. The Church shows us our history and how we fit into the life of Christ. She takes the long view, always with the knowledge that she is a Church in motion, a Church on the way.

Mother Church is on a pilgrimage to heaven. It is a pilgrimage with our family on earth to journey to meet the rest of the extended family in heaven. Our Mother's joy is to ultimately bring us to the Father, so we see him face-to-face. No matter what part of the journey they are on, children can cling to this mother so they do not become lost.

Mother Church seeks to embrace the entire world with arms of love and truth. I often think of the symbolism behind the architecture we find in the two "arms" of the colonnade that reach out from St. Peter's Basilica in Rome. They create St. Peter's Square—which is not a square at all! Rather, from above it looks like a mother's encircling embrace of the children and pilgrims who come to visit the mother of all churches in Vatican City. Gian Lorenzo Bernini, who designed the colonnade in the seventeenth century, said that St. Peter's portico "had to give an open-armed, maternal welcome."[14]

The Church is mother *and* teacher. She hands on to generations the words and deeds—the message—of her Beloved Jesus. "The Church . . . faithfully guards . . . the memory of Christ's words; it is she who from generation to generation hands on the apostles' confession of faith. As a mother who teaches her children to speak and so to understand and communicate, the Church our Mother . . . introduce[s] us to . . . the life of faith" (*CCC*, 171).

The Church's teaching is not only for her own children—those who are baptized—but Jesus equipped the Church's motherhood for a bigger mission: to tell the whole world of her Beloved Spouse. She is a teacher to the nations.

St. John XXIII taught, "Mother and Teacher of all nations—such is the Catholic Church in the mind of her Founder, Jesus Christ; to hold the world in an embrace of love, that [human persons], in every age, should find in her their own completeness in a higher order of living, and their ultimate salvation. She is '*the pillar and ground of the truth*' (cf. 1 Tm 3:15)."[15]

Children of God need the embrace of their Mother Church to live a virtuous life and attain heaven. Those who have yet to experience the family of God may look to the worldwide embrace of this universal mother. Her arms remain open.

BECOMING THE BELOVED CHILD, REVISITED

All this talk about being a child of God may seem rather, um, childish. I mean, we're grown adults, so why all this about being a child and needing a mother?

Sometimes we need the quiet humility to say that we don't know it all, that there is more to know. There are some things that only God knows, and there are some that he chose to reveal through his Son and his Church.

Paul Claudel, the twentieth-century French diplomat, playwright, essayist, and poet nominated for the Nobel Prize for literature many times, described his conversion with these few words: "Praised be this great, majestic Mother, at whose knees I have learned everything!"[16]

We can choose to mature in the spiritual life as we do in our natural life. We must grow up in our union with Christ—to have an adult faith, while being ever mindful of the gift of our spiritual childhood. Jesus taught, "Truly I tell you, unless you change and become like children, you will never enter the kingdom of heaven. Whoever becomes humble like this child is the greatest in the kingdom of heaven" (Mt 18:3–4).

This seems a conundrum, but I've taken heart in the explanation from Jesuit theologian Henri de Lubac, who offers insight into this education we need in being children of God: "The more the Christian becomes an adult in Christ . . . the more also does the spirit of childhood blossom within him, as Jesus understands it. Or, if you prefer, it is a deepening of this childlike spirit that the Christian advances to adulthood, penetrating ever deeper, if we can put it this way, into the womb of his mother."[17] Using the language of faith, de Lubac furthers the point that as we grow and mature in the faith, we don't cut ties with our mother and leave home or, to be specific, leave the womb of Mother Church. In this way we attain the "greatness" of little children, as Jesus taught, while we mature into an adult faith. Jesus prayed, "I thank you, Father, . . . because you have hidden these things from the wise and the intelligent and have revealed them to infants" (Mt 11:25). De Lubac continues, "Perhaps, however, we can try to glimpse something of it. In our natural life, in fact, each step toward adulthood is a move away from childhood; it is like a loss of paradise, a step toward old age and decrepitude. But in *the spiritual life, on the contrary, all progress is, in the proper sense, a renewal.* It is an increase in vitality, it is one more step taking within a substantial newness and consequently always new."[18]

To be a child of God is to learn to live with ongoing conversion, ongoing renewal. We are not going backward; we are being ever renewed. Paradoxically, we can fully become an adult while remaining fully a child. This keeps our faith fresh and alive—or, to borrow a phrase from St. Augustine, "ever ancient, ever new."

The young Catholic woman clapping and clamoring to see the pope in person at Madison Square Garden is the same person writing this today. From a calendar standpoint, 1979 seems like ancient history. But the spark that lights my faith is ever new every morning. That pope looking across the arena is now a saint of the Church looking down from heaven. This woman is now a confident daughter of God the Father and of Mary and of Mother Church.

I'm so happy to be related to a global and heavenly family. And I can't wait to meet my big brother in faith, "JP2," in person—Lord willing—someday in heaven.

Pray

Honor the Blessed Virgin Mary by praying the Rosary. She desires to be your spiritual mother. If you need to learn how to pray the Rosary, go to http://rosaryarmy. newevangelizers.com.

Learn

When it comes to understanding the Church, I recommend that all Catholics read *Lumen Gentium*, the Dogmatic Constitution of the Church from Vatican II. However, for now, if you just wish to focus on Mary, read paragraphs 52–69 of that document. Find it at the Vatican website: http://www.vatican.va/archive/hist_councils/ii_vatican_council/documents/vat-ii_const_19641121_lumen-gentium_en.html.

Or read Pope John Paul II's encyclical *Redemptoris Mater*. It's all about Mary, the Mother of the Redeemer. Don't have time for the whole thing? Skip to paragraphs 42–47. Find it at the Vatican website: http://w2.vatican. va/content/john-paul-ii/en/encyclicals/documents/hf_jp-ii_enc_25031987_redemptoris-mater.html.

Engage

Discover a new saint or two to help you love and trust Mary and the Church. Explore the quotations and writings of these saints who were known for great devotion to Mary and to the Church.

St. Louis de Montfort

St. Alphonsus Ligouri

St. Bernard of Clairvaux

St. Thérèse of Lisieux

St. Maximilian Kolbe
St. John Paul II
St. Teresa of Calcutta

CHAPTER 6

THE
DIVINE FRIEND

A TOEHOLD

I'm no fan of MRI tubes.[1] With my cancer history, diagnostic tests are routine, so I've had many MRI sessions in hospital radiology labs. I'd prep for the exam, lie on the table, put the earplugs in (it's noisy in the tube!), and slide on the conveyer into the tube. I'd close my eyes and relax as best I could as the narrow walls cocooned me.

I never experienced claustrophobia in the MRI until the year my medical team decided we needed to "watch something" near the center of my brain. That meant three more MRIs that would be more "involved" than past ones. Besides the customary hospital gown, a troubling accessory was added. My head would be strapped down to the table and my face covered with a close-fitting shield. Head movements, I was told, would ruin the giant magnet's images and force retakes. How nonchalantly I was reminded to hold very still for "about an hour" as I was handed a "panic button" to hold "for an emergency."

I freaked out a little in that first session. My skittishness progressed to an anxious claustrophobic state. I could feel my breath rushing around the mask, fogging it, and

forming tears on my eyelashes. Usually a confident, sea-
soned patient when taking exams, I was reduced to being
a baby. I was pretty shaky when they brought me out. I
learned that claustrophobia is real, and I wished I had
brought someone with me.

The thought of enduring two more MRIs in the coming months gave me pause. I could not be medicated to
sleep through them, so I did the next best thing and asked
Bob to join me.

Rounds two and three in the year-of-watching-
if-something-ominous-is-growing-in-my-brain were
somewhat better. Bob was my anxiety medicine. He had
seen me through childbirth, cancer, and lots in between.
He's a steady person in a tight spot, claustrophobic pun
notwithstanding.

The hospital staff made the kind concession of allowing Bob in the MRI lab with me. But not before he had the
prescreening check, signed a release, and left all metal on
his clothes or in his pockets behind. They prepped me,
strapped on my headgear, and wheeled me into the tube.
I took deep breaths and tried not to cry.

Only my toes stuck out of the tube. Bob sat in a chair
next to the opening where only my feet were. He was
allowed to hold my toes. That's all he could do for me.
For an hour.

Hunched over, arm extended, Bob held on to my toes
and tapped my sole in a kind of loving Morse code. He
couldn't get inside the tube with me, but he was present.
He joined my suffering and silently prayed. As a longtime married couple we've experienced deep intimacy and
moments of marital harmony, but *this*? This little sacrifice
of accompanying me and holding my feet offered sublime
comfort.

Bob repeated his toe-touching exercise a few months
later. Twelve months after I started, the specialists released
me. Whatever was lighting up on their screens and causing

their suspicions was "likely normal" for me since "it" never changed in a year—that and, I suppose, the fact it hadn't killed me.

I thank God every day for my best friend and confidante, Bob. Through the years, the trials and the good stuff wrought an intense relationship that has grown deeper with time. We've learned in big ways and small how "to lay down one's life for one's friend" (Jn 15:13).

We've field-tested every wedding vow. We've been rich. We've been poor. We've seen each other through sickness (and lots of diagnostics!) and, gratefully, experienced good health, too. We've been blessed by good times and stayed faithful in the bad times.

Through it all, we've held each other's hands—and *feet*!

"Who Do You Say That I Am?"

There's an abiding comfort that exists between good friends. It comes with time. You've moved to that place where just being in one another's presence brings joy and freedom, even when no words are spoken. You are at home with one another, and you love to serve each other.

A life with Christ is meant to display that quality of friendship. The Catholic Church has long proposed that in the spiritual life we develop in greater intimacy with the One who already knows our hearts best. Being a Catholic is not about having information about Jesus but experiencing transformation in him!

We're called not only to know about Jesus but to know him *personally*. I'm reminded of this exchange between Jesus and his apostles. "Now when Jesus came into the district of Caesarea Philippi, he asked his disciples, 'Who do people say that the Son of Man is?' And they said, 'Some say John the Baptist, but others Elijah, and still others Jeremiah or one of the prophets.' He said to them, 'But who do you say that I am?' Simon Peter answered, 'You are the

Messiah, the Son of the living God'" (Mt 16:13–16). Jesus' second question—*"Who do you say that I am?"*— laid it on the line. Each Christian through history must confront the heart of matter: Who is Jesus for *me?*

Do I have a personal relationship with Jesus? Have I decided to follow him?

Yes and yes.

I was prepared for my relationship with Jesus by the lessons I learned from my parents and my Catholic religious education. Jesus already had a relationship with me, thanks to the sacraments I had received. But I did not really return that love wholeheartedly until those earliest encounters with Jesus—my experiences in prayer and in scripture—when I *knew* I had *met* the Lord. Those moments were *heart* knowledge, not head knowledge. They were turning points for me when I decided to follow Jesus more closely.

My life with Jesus was a slow burn, a friendship that grew over time. His divine friendship called me to participate in the community of my local church. He wanted me to form relationships with members of his Body and to have Mother Church nurture me and school me in her wisdom.

Who do you say that I am, Pat?

You are my Lord and my God, and I want to be your friend and follower.

Pope Benedict XVI preached about this question that Jesus still asks today:

> So Jesus' question—*"But who do you say that I am?"*—
> is ultimately a challenge to the disciples to make a
> personal decision in his regard. Faith in Christ and
> discipleship are tightly interconnected.
>
> And since faith involves following the Master,
> it must become constantly stronger and deeper, and
> more mature to the extent that it leads to a closer and
> more intense relationship with Jesus. Peter and the

other disciples also had to grow in this way, until
their encounter with the risen Lord opened their eyes
to the fullness of faith.[2]

My love for Jesus today includes an all-in love for his
Church. I have deep affection for Jesus' friends, especially
the beloved disciple, John. Yet my affinity for Peter is just
as great—so much so that Bob and I named a son after him.

Peter's bold answer—"You are the Messiah, the Son
of the living God"—was a gift of grace born from his deepening relationship with Jesus. Then Jesus responded with
an even bigger gift for Peter. "Jesus answered him, 'Blessed
are you, Simon son of Jonah! For flesh and blood has not
revealed this to you, but my Father in heaven. And I tell
you, you are Peter, and on this rock I will build my church,
and the gates of Hades will not prevail against it. I will give
you the keys of the kingdom of heaven, and whatever you
bind on earth will be bound in heaven, and whatever you
loose on earth will be loosed in heaven'" (Mt 16:17–19).

What a moment for Peter! Scripture scholars see this
scene as Peter's elevation as the first pope, the leader of
the nascent Church that would spread the message of
the kingdom of God. Jesus is the King of this kingdom,
and Peter would be his prime minister. The keys are the
authority that Jesus invests in Peter to lead and govern.
The powerful gift Peter received was a great gift destined
to bless all of us. Here we discover that "the Church, then,
is not simply a human institution. . . . She is closely joined
to God. Christ himself speaks of her as 'his' Church. Christ
cannot be separated from the Church any more than the
head can be separated from the body (cf. 1 Cor 12:12)."[3]

Yet there are other moments in Peter's life that show
that moving toward union with Jesus, and toward the fullness of faith that Jesus desires for us, can be a twisty road.
Not because of what Jesus does, of course, but because of
what we do.

Those who've studied Peter's life recall that Peter, the would-be pope, had some inglorious moments. Soon after Jesus' arrest, Peter denied Jesus not once but three times! A vibrant supporter and friend of Jesus, Peter turned a coward when his best friend was on trial for his life! (See Jn 15:18, 25–26.)

Yet Jesus is ever faithful. Jesus, as he suffered on the Cross, forgave Peter, along with every other sinner in the world, past, present, and to come.

After his resurrection, Jesus' relationship with Peter was also raised from the dead. The beloved disciple was a witness to their reconciliation. John's gospel shows that Jesus doesn't hold a grudge; instead, he raises Peter up.

> When they had finished breakfast, Jesus said to Simon Peter, "Simon son of John, do you love me more than these?" He said to him, "Yes, Lord; you know that I love you." Jesus said to him, "Feed my lambs." A second time he said to him, "Simon son of John, do you love me?" He said to him, "Yes, Lord; you know that I love you." Jesus said to him, "Tend my sheep." He said to him the third time, "Simon son of John, do you love me?" Peter felt hurt because he said to him the third time, "Do you love me?" And he said to him, "Lord, you know everything; you know that I love you." Jesus said to him, "Feed my sheep. Very truly, I tell you, when you were younger, you used to fasten your own belt and to go wherever you wished. But when you grow old, you will stretch out your hands, and someone else will fasten a belt around you and take you where you do not wish to go." (He said this to indicate the kind of death by which he would glorify God.) After this he said to him, "Follow me." (Jn 21:15–19)

Peter declares his love for Jesus three times. In case you haven't noticed, this is Peter going all in for Jesus.

Jesus allows Peter to clear the air between them regarding his thrice-denial, in case there were any lingering doubts. Jesus knows that Peter will lay his life down for him.

Jesus offers us the same mercy, even when we feel pretty sheepish about our past mistakes. He wants us to put away any excuses about building, or rebuilding, our relationship with him.

If Jesus can have patience and forbearance with Peter, he will do the same for us. Pope Francis, in a homily reflecting on Peter's relationship with Jesus, observed it as "a long road, a road of grace and sin, a disciple's road."[4]

So what's it going to be for you? Where are you on the road?

Is your heart busy denying that Jesus could love you, given all you've done wrong?

Can you see yourself becoming a friend to Jesus, a disciple?

Have you made a conscious decision to follow Jesus? Or are you on the fence?

MERCY AND GRACE

Today, I know Jesus not only as my friend but as my healer, my redeemer, and my deliverer. He has accompanied me through some scary times and through the best of times.

Good friends always want what's best for us, even if it means confronting the things we need to change. That's how Jesus works in my life. His love that I receive, especially in the Eucharist, gives me the confidence to change. His compassionate love wins me over, allowing him to "clean house" in the home he is making in me. Through the sacrament of Reconciliation, Jesus helps me rip sin out by its roots. Have no doubt we're still working on some things, but he's given me a better way to live than I could have found on my own. That's what his friends discover about him and his Church—a better way to live and to love.

Jesus desires us to live the life of the Spirit, whom Jesus called the promise of the Father (see Lk 24:59).

The first gift the Holy Spirit brings is conversion—to turn our hearts toward Jesus and away from sin. After experiencing mercy and redemption in Christ, we are called to a life of ongoing renewal. Graces are supplied by the Holy Spirit to do that, both directly in certain moments and by the Spirit's power in the sacraments.

Our spiritual progress depends on our growing in a closer union with God.

Mercy and grace help us get there.

God's mercy is his compassionate, forgiving love— like the kind he extended to Peter and so many others, for "all have sinned and fall short of the glory of God"(Rom 3:23).

God knows we are weak and needy. His mercy is the remedy, the antidote for all that ails us. His mercy is a true gift. We can't earn it. We're unable to manufacture the very thing we need the most. Only Jesus can give us mercy. It is freely bestowed on loved sinners.

We see mercy in operation in the gospels. In the life of Jesus, mercy is quickly dispensed, especially for those who just ask him. Mercy was a gift to the woman at the well, the woman caught in adultery, the leper, the demoniac, the woman whose son died, the friends of Lazarus, the man born blind, the woman with a hemorrhage, the tax collector, the prostitute, the lost, the lame, and so many more folks that resemble you and me.

Mercy converts us. An acute problem for many of us is we don't really understand our need of mercy. We rely on ourselves to a fault. We are so used to being our own support, our own supply—or having the means to buy or barter for what we need. We, in a way, have become our own god or have been trusting cheap substitutes.

Mercy is for those who are done with that.

Mercy is for those who say, *I cannot do this on my own*. And it's a good thing because believing we are all alone, and behaving as if it all depends on us, is our first big mistake.

Mercy is a coming home to the understanding that we need the presence of God.

When we come to Jesus to receive his mercy, he freely gives it to us. Then he sends more graces to strengthen us, that we may live a life that reflects his goodness to us—and so that we may be merciful to others.

Grace, another gift from God, follows in mercy's footsteps.

Do you really know what grace is? And what it does?

Grace is God's favor, a sharing in his divine life; it is supernatural—divine help or aid.

I've mentioned this before: what Jesus is by nature, we are called to be by grace. Grace builds on our nature. We need grace like we need oxygen. It keeps the life of the Spirit alive in us. No matter what our pride says or what our perfectionism demands, it is a lie to think we do not need the Holy Spirit or his benevolent graces.

Just like mercy, we cannot make or buy grace—it is a pure gift. We don't achieve grace; we receive it. We don't control grace, but we can choose to be open to it or not.

Humans cannot make what is divine. But we can receive it, know it, and live in cooperation with it. Call it yielding to the divine or being obedient to God's grace rather than to ourselves or to any of the little false gods we make for ourselves. This is St. Paul's tribute to the grace we find in Christ and in the Church:

> But God, who is rich in mercy, out of the great love with which he loved us even when we were dead through our trespasses, made us alive together with Christ—by grace you have been saved— and raised us up with him and seated us with him in the

heavenly places in Christ Jesus, so that in the ages to come he might show the immeasurable riches of his grace in kindness toward us in Christ Jesus. For by grace you have been saved through faith, and this is not your own doing; it is the gift of God—not the result of works, so that no one may boast. For we are what he has made us, created in Christ Jesus for good works, which God prepared beforehand to be our way of life. (Eph 2:4–10)

One negative effect of sin in our lives is the dullness it brings—dulling the eyes of faith. Our spiritual vision is impaired. We cannot see the true brightness of grace's glory and gifts. Sin dulls our minds; it lulls us into thinking that nothing can be done for us. It's hopeless, making us think, *That's just the way life is, like it or lump it.*

No.

Grace says no.

Grace says no to your negative thinking. For grace is God's holy yes that you *can* live a life of union with Jesus and with others.

Sin drains. Grace gains.

Sin tames me and shames me. Grace inflames and reframes me.

Sin retains me. Grace unchains me, and grace retrains me.

Sin knocks me down. Grace raises me up.

Sin plunges. Grace expunges.

Sin destroys. Grace gives joys.

Let us choose to move away from sin, to turn and beg Jesus for the grace to begin again.

Yes! Begin again! That's the motto of all the saints. Saints were once sinners who knew they are loved—and didn't quit! They stayed open to grace! They reformed themselves to the shape of grace—the grace that, by the Spirit's power, conforms them to be more like Christ.

So add one more to the growing list of grace's goodness.

Sin deforms. Grace *transforms.*

How can we be so confident in this potent power of grace?

Where does this grace come from?

It comes from the blood Jesus shed for us on the Cross.

Jesus died for our sins.

Jesus died to release us from the choke hold of sin— the blockade to receiving all the gifts he wants to lavish on us.

On the Cross, Jesus smashed to bits every sin, fault, failing, and vice that arrests us, taunts us, or defeats us. We no longer have to suffer being chained by invisible shackles. His sacrifice releases the graces we need to be freed from sin and death and shame.

There is power in his blood.

Again, the beloved disciple captures this truth: "The blood of Jesus . . . cleanses us from all sin" (1 Jn 1:7). By the merits of Jesus' Cross, we are redeemed.

A large part of my early years with Jesus was spent reveling in the Divine Friend. I was remiss in not fully appreciating how important Jesus' death was for me personally. Of course Jesus wanted to give me his love, and I wanted to give him mine in return. But I didn't want the cross. It was too hard, too terrible.

When I went on a retreat as a teenager and got to know Jesus, I was all about his friendship and love. It filled a void in me that only Jesus could. The benefits of my healed heart, coupled with the friendship of Jesus and the friends I had in the local church, made me feel rich indeed. Yet I had not fully considered the depths to which Jesus descended to bring me that love.

I needed maturing. I took Jesus' love for granted and did not realize that by ignoring the role of his suffering and death for me; I behaved like Easter Sunday happened without the pains of Good Friday. I might as well have been Peter denying Jesus to his face, not realizing the necessity of his Cross for my redemption.

For years I missed the full impact and truth of what Jesus had done for me. It also affected my reception of Holy Communion. I saw it as holy food that Jesus gave me as sustenance—while it is that it is also more. It is also a sacrifice provided by his suffering and dying for me.

Suffering in my own life changed all of that. I didn't know real suffering until I got older—physical suffering, emotional suffering, and spiritual suffering. The list of my own pains was long; the lists of sorrows that family and friends suffered were even longer.

For me there was a traumatic birth and a tough initiation into motherhood, an out-of-state move that affected me deeply, and several friends lost to cancer. There was the demise of a strong church community that fell apart over the sex-abuse scandals. There was the breakup of good friends' marriages. Who could have predicted the traumas of 9/11 and the wars that followed? So much pain and loss.

One little phrase from the Church's Evening Prayer begs Jesus that we believers might "see in your passion our suffering." By uniting my suffering to Christ's passion I survive. By the merits and graces of his Cross I thrive.

By grace I have been saved.

Once again, the Incarnation plays an indispensable role in our salvation.

The Incarnation unites the God of heaven to humanity, to earthly people of dust.

We are made of dust, the Bible says (see Gn 3:19). Yet the Father God loves the very dust we are.

> As a father has compassion for his children,
>   so the LORD has compassion for those who fear
>   him.
>   For he knows how we were made;
> he remembers that we are dust. (Ps 103:13–14)

The Father sends the Son, and Jesus sanctifies our dust and makes it holy. The dust we are, thanks to God's compassion for us, is made for more. I think of Pigpen, the character from the *Peanuts* comic strips. Pigpen could not avoid dust and dirt, yet he also made peace with being dusty. Sometimes we've grown a bit too accustomed to the mess we are. We become complacent, settled in our own dust.

Pope Benedict XVI taught that we are made for more. "Man was created for greatness—for God himself; he was created to be filled by God. But his heart is too small for the greatness to which it is destined. It must be stretched. . . . This requires hard work . . . but in this way alone do we become suited to that for which we are destined."[5] We are made for transformation.

Enter Jesus, the dust-loving God-man whose power redeems us and, quite literally, dusts us off and breathes new life—the destiny of eternal life—into our dust.

This is God's plan of sheer goodness! This is not merited nor earned by us. This truth and goodness I've come to know, at last, is that my glorious Lord lowered himself to enter my dusty, musty, rusty, crusty existence so that he might raise me up. What dignity I have found in this love, this mercy, this grace.

Sheer grace.

IT'S TIME TO PRAY

We are all sinners. The question is, what to do about it?

Jesus already conquered our sins. He saves us.

Only one thing comes to my mind if this is all news to you: ask for Jesus' forgiveness, and receive the mercy he can't wait to give you, no strings attached.

If you feel moved to do so, take a few moments to pause and pray.

Jesus, I trust in you. Send me your mercy. I'm sorry
I've sinned against you. The incarnation weds you,
Lord, to every human person—and to me—and weds
your suffering to me and mine to yours.

I'm sorry I've not understood the depths of
my sinfulness before now, nor your sufferings that
brought me salvation in the kingdom of God. Your
blood beats in my brokenness and bleeding. Your
blood redeems my life.

Besides your healing mercy, allow your Holy
Spirit to send me your abundant graces that I may
live the divine life and be more closely united to you
and my Father in heaven.

I ask for the grace to love you more and more
every day of my life, to go all in. Keep me close to
your Church, that I may never be far from the graces
you wish to supply. Guard me and keep me, Jesus,
as one of your beloved disciples. Amen.

Through prayer and active participation in the Catholic Church, I continue to know, love, and serve Jesus. He
is real. He is not someone *from* history—he is the Lord *of*
history. He is the King of Glory through whom everything
was made. Jesus and I have a history together. We talk
together every day in prayer. I'm confident he's the one
with me in the tight places, in the deepest places in my
soul that no one else can see. Where his love is, fear fades
and hope grows.

The Church, in her motherly wisdom, always proposes that we need this relationship, this encounter with
God. She never imposes it. A life with God is a free gift
and a free choice. Yet the Church stands to remind us that
God loved us first. God makes the first move. The Church's
existence is a response to that first love.

The Catholic Church is the result of God's initiative.
Jesus is her founder and Spouse. The Church is *his*.

From girlhood to my middle age, Jesus has been with me in every season. His presence is everywhere, but I know it especially when I pray—quietly in the mornings, with my family, at my desk at work, in the car when I drive, or at Mass.

Yes, I felt lonely and frightened in that MRI machine when I suffered claustrophobia. Loneliness is a feeling, a temporary emotional state. Other emotional and psychological conditions, such as depression, can cause great bouts of loneliness. Yet we are never truly alone because God is never absent.

With Christ living in me, I am never alone. Ever.

St. Paul assures us that "anyone united to the Lord becomes one spirit with him" (1 Cor 6:17).

Additionally, as a member of the Body of Christ, I am part of a worldwide community on earth and in heaven. Belonging to the Catholic Church showers us with the presence of others and, most significantly, the presence of God. God's desire to have a home in us is real. The more we welcome him, the more we are in union with God. That's how intimacy works. It is a slow unveiling of oneself before the one we trust.

A GOD WITH TOES

Like a marriage hewn from sacrifices of time and commitment, it is the day-to-day awareness of one another, and regular conversation, that helps our loving friendship with Jesus to grow. Catholics call those conversations with God *prayer*.

For several years now, I've made a weekly holy hour. It's my weekly appointment with God. Most Friday afternoons you'll find me at the church where I am a regular adorer of the presence of Jesus in the Blessed Sacrament. At adoration, I sit or kneel and face Jesus, the Divine Friend, present in the host. We talk.

Above the monstrance, the vessel with the host, a statue depicts the risen Jesus. His arms are outstretched, with the wounds of crucifixion still visible. Once-crucified feet extend low into my field of vision, inches from the monstrance, as I concentrate on his presence in the host.

Whenever I enter the chapel, this all comes into view. My knees hit the floor and I bend low, praying: *My Lord and my God!*

Not insignificantly, my Lord and my God has toes.

As I gaze upon Jesus in the Eucharist, I find that this God, undeniably magnificent as the Creator of the cosmos, is, in his humanity, very much loved by my down-to-earth sensibilities.

We have a God with toes. Isn't *that* amazing?

Taking a page or two from my prayer journal, indulge me as I share my meditations on Jesus' toes:

> One afternoon with the Blessed Sacrament, I saw those toes and my own mother's heart revved into high gear. I mused about the Babe of Bethlehem, born to Momma Mary and Joseph. Those young parents treasured those ten toes. I picture Mary's motherly kisses on newborn feet, lavishing him from head to toe!
>
> And then I'm thinking of another woman and her lavishing love of Jesus. The gospel tells us she was so transformed by the love of this God-made-man—this God with toes—that she bathed his feet with her tears, anointed them with oil, drying them with her hair (see Lk 7:37–38).
>
> In the next moment, my mind's eye catches glimpses of those holy feet covered in dust and blood, bearing the weight of a cross beam, marching relentlessly to Calvary. Executioners would mercilessly pin his feet to the wood.
>
> With Jesus raised on that Cross, I contemplate Mary standing before those aching, wounded

feet—perhaps the only part of him reachable to her motherly touch (see Jn 19:25–27).

Echoes of that Good Friday remain with me as I gaze at the Eucharist before me. Now it is my turn, woman that I am, to lean in and adore the feet of him whom I desire to know so well . . . the Redeemer who removes all my sin and shame in such a kiss.

And all at once, I am a mother delighting, and a sinner confessing, and a believer rejoicing in the gift of these feet, these toes.

Regular adoration of the Blessed Sacrament has helped me grow closer to Christ. *All* of us were made for union and communion with God. *This!* This was God's idea before the world began. It's why we long for connections and why we get our hearts broken when our human loves fall short. Our hearts are restless until they rest in the only heart big enough to hold them for eternity—the Sacred Heart of Jesus, the Beloved. Without Jesus coming as a human person, I wouldn't enjoy the *grace upon grace* that he died to give me.

Jesus is the Divine Friend who went all in for you. He loves you from the top of your head to the bottom of your toes.

PRAY

Using a Bible, meditate on John 15:1–17.

LEARN

Read about the power of the blood of Jesus in the *Catechism of the Catholic Church*. See paragraphs 517, 610, 787, 808, 827, 1384, 1432, 1442, and 1992.

ENGAGE

Visit a Catholic church and sit before the Real Presence of Jesus. He is found in the tabernacle, where a sanctuary candle is lit.

Even better, if a local church offers adoration of the Blessed Sacrament, where the Blessed Sacrament is exposed in silence, try to make a holy hour with Jesus.

Pray silently in your own words with Jesus, or begin praying the prayer we prayed together in this chapter. You can also bring a Bible and pray with any of the scriptures recommended in this book. Just remember that Jesus is there with you in the adoration chapel in a most sublime way. You are not alone.

CHAPTER 7

THE MYSTICAL
BODY OF CHRIST

SHARING IN THE LIGHT

Come for dinner, and you'll find the table aglow with candlelight every night. It might be the fancy candlesticks at holidays and special occasions, or it might be a simple pillar candle set in glass. I'm not trying to add romance; with this little ritual, I'm recalling an important connection. We light our candle in all seasons to remind us that the light of Christ is always with us—he is the unseen guest, the one who is always present. Hidden within that faith in Christ's presence is an even greater mystery: we are joined not only to Christ but to the entire family of God in the Mystical Body of Christ.

During the Easter season, Catholic churches light the paschal candle (sometimes called a Christ candle or Easter candle) symbolizing Christ's light and presence in our worship and prayers. So too with our candle at our family table do we remember Jesus and our link to the Body of Christ.

When each of my children left for college, I told them we would remember them around this table every night. We would see them in this light, thanks to our belonging to the Body of Christ. Our hearts would be connected through Christ. The same holds true for our relatives and loved ones near and far.

If you've never been to the Easter Vigil on the Saturday night before Easter Sunday, don't miss it next time. From its holy fire burning outside the church to the procession of the paschal candle into a darkened church to its carefully selected scriptures recalling the promises of salvation history, the coming of Jesus, the Messiah, and his resurrection from the dead, it is a dramatic and stirring crescendo after the penitential practices of Lent and Holy Week.

The Easter Vigil liturgy welcomes newly baptized members and those receiving sacraments of initiation. It's a powerful opportunity for us to publicly renew our profession of faith. When we finally get to the celebration of the Eucharist, the sacrament that seals our unity and feeds our souls, the Easter joy is palpable.

Every Mass offers indications that we belong to the Mystical Body of Christ. One vivid symbol, unique to the Vigil, is the initial lighting and procession of the paschal candle. Allow me to narrate the experience I have had while taking part in the Easter Vigil.

The Vigil begins on Holy Saturday night, in the dark. A large fire is lit outside of the church and is blessed by the priest. The fire symbolizes our hope of eternal life. The fire is the source of the paschal candle's flame. The candle will be used throughout the Easter season Masses and is an important symbol at baptisms and funerals throughout the year.

The paschal candle is a tall pillar set in an ornate candlestick to match its size and weight. It is usually the largest candle in a church—to convey the truth that Christ is the light of the world, just as he said: "I am the light of the world. Whoever follows me will never walk in darkness but will have the light of life" (Jn 8:12).

The purity of the candle's beeswax reminds us of Christ's sinless purity. The wick of the candle represents his humanity. The flame of the candle represents his divinity. Inscribed onto the paschal candle are the symbols of a cross, an alpha and omega (in Greek, "the beginning and the end" [see Rv 22:13]), and the numerals of the current year. The priest prays that the light of Christ, rising in glory, may dispel the darkness of our hearts and minds. He affixes five grains of incense to the candle, representing the wounds Jesus suffered on his hands, feet, and side.

Imagine what takes place next—the procession of the paschal candle—as a picture of what happens in our souls when we encounter Jesus Christ. There is movement from dark to light, a before-and-after story. A light comes, and a joy warms us. It is a light that will be shared with others.

The procession moves from the holy fire into the darkened church with a priest (or deacon) strong enough to hold the giant candle aloft. This symbolism reminds us of Jesus coming from the light of heaven into the darkness of a world troubled by sin and pain. All that holy fire, all the power of God in eternity, is now shielded from our eyes yet revealed in a Savior with human flesh. Jesus' light—"the light of the world" (Jn 8:12, 9:5)—has moved through the ages, until it has reached us.

The priest moves the paschal candle slowly to different locations within the church chanting, "Christ, our Light!" The gathered congregation replies, "Thanks be to God!" People in darkness are grateful for sunlight. A person drowning knows the joy of a life raft. After a Lent of fasting, almsgiving, and prayer—trying to do away with sin—we long for God whose light is our rescue.

After each acclamation and response, the paschal candle is lowered briefly to allow others to light tapers from it. In our encounter with Christ, we draw some of his own light and life into our own lives. We no longer suffer in darkness.

These individual candles are powerful reminders of Baptism. Jesus met us in that first sacrament. The candle we received at our baptisms (or that was handed to our parents or godparents if we were infants) was lit from the church's paschal candle on the day of our baptisms. When we were baptized, we were formed in the likeness of Christ. "For in the one Spirit we were all baptized into one body" (1 Cor 12:13).

Slowly, in repetition, as Jesus is proclaimed and the procession continues with the paschal candle held aloft, the light of Christ is symbolically spread throughout the church. Eventually each member holds a taper candle that has been lit either from the Christ candle itself or from another person's candle that has shared the light. This demonstrates our common faith and the call to spread it. Later in the Mass we renew our baptismal promises. On most Sundays we do this by praying the Creed aloud together. But on Easter, we renew those promises carefully, one by one.

As the procession concludes, darkness has faded and the church is illuminated by warm candlelight. The light from the flame each person carries shines on every face. The one light of the paschal candle never diminishes even as its flame is shared creating new lights. This powerful moment symbolically captures our own conversion, or turning toward the light when we encounter the true light of Christ. And it is at once personal and corporate for we all share the same faith, the same flame of the Spirit! This is the light of faith that we must bring to others.

The paschal candle is then set down in a prominent location within the church. We have acclaimed the centrality of our faith in Christ, who is "the Light of the nations."[1] He is the light of our local church and the light of every human heart.

Beautiful as all this symbolism is, it is meant to draw us deeper in preparation for the rest of the Mass. Soon to come is a more powerful and compelling reality, the actual proof and source of our union with Christ and one another: the Eucharist, the Body and Blood of the Lord. This risen Lord is alive in the Eucharist and alive in those who receive him. His call to us is to live in union with him and the Church, so we might make disciples of all the nations.

THREE STATES

Why does the Catholic Church use the word *mystical* to describe the Body of Christ? Is it magical? Or a mystery? The term is actually a description that the Church uses to indicate its *full* membership as a society of baptized believers, together with the pope and hierarchy, in union with the saints in heaven and the souls of purgatory. This is the entirety of the Church from the past and in the present. That's worthy of our consideration.

The Splendor of the Church is not her cathedrals or schools of higher learning, her great art or music, or even the Bible. (Now, good reader, I'm not dissing any of those wondrous things. Let's just say they are all splendorous with a small *s*.)

The Splendor of the Church is in her Lord Jesus Christ, in union with her saints! I'm talking about all saints from throughout the ages who populate heaven and those saints in the making in purgatory—and one day, too, Lord willing, aspiring saints like you and me.

There are, therefore, three states of the Church.

Do you remember learning that when Alaska joined the United States it added an impressive twenty percent to the size of our nation's landmass? Well, learning about the three states of the Church is like that, only more staggering. Do you recall how the Church is both human and divine? It's a dynamic church! Understanding it is akin to realizing that the most amazing and formidable part of the iceberg is the part you don't see under the water!

The biggest part of the Church is still hidden from our view! Sometimes this leaves us thinking too little of the Church. Not a chance, once you know about these three states of the Church.

The first state is all those saints living in heaven with the Lord—they are known as the Church Triumphant. These members of the Body already have their heavenly reward. There are more saints in heaven than we realize. We have to think of all the saints who could be there since the time that humans walked the earth because Jesus' Cross won the victory for all the generations that preceded his, not just all who came after—like us.

The second state are those Christians still living out their lives on earth right now. They are called the Church Militant, because they are still fighting "the good fight of the faith" (1 Tm 6:12). We are the smallest Church sojourning toward the full light of God.

Finally there is the Church Suffering—that is, those whose reward is heaven, but it's a bit delayed because they are still being purified in purgatory. This is not a second chance to get to heaven. They've already made the cut. But they still need "a final cleansing of human imperfection before one is able to enter the joy of heaven."[2] My money is on a pretty sizable population of the Church living in this state. Just think of all the Christians dying in a day—or in a month or in a year—in all the years since you were born. Think they all passed "Go" and collected $200? I'm guessing that, in the Lord's mercy, many are still on "Go" and waiting for their turn to advance.

I like to think of purgatory as heaven's welcome mat. You're at the door of heaven, but Dad says first *ya gotta wipe ya feet* before you come in! Purgatory purges a soul from the residue of sins. Each November the Church has a whole month dedicated to praying for holy souls. That's a lot of praying, so there's probably a bazillion souls who need sprucing up before entering the Father's house. So offer a prayer for them whenever you think of it.

These three states remind us why the Church is different from any other group or community. The Church invests in the eternal destiny of her members, helping them become more and more like the Beloved.

The Church uses the word *mystical* to indicate that the Body that is the Church *transcends* what we normally associate with human structures and institutions. The Church is both human and divine—that is her mystery.

Belonging to the Mystical Body of Christ leads to transformation.

Belonging to a club, organization, or some other human group cannot hold a candle to our belonging to the Church. In those groups, one might pay dues for membership and agree to the bylaws, set up by members, that are subject to change over time. Human institutions do not have the spiritual nature that comes from having a divine founder and spiritual benefits, including the membership freely given in Baptism. Belonging to the Church means belonging to Jesus Christ, and that belonging is ratified in Baptism and the graces of the sacramental life. All that grace brings about positive changes in the very human persons we are—it equips us for heaven!

While the Church may indeed have certain external and internal hierarchical structures that appear to human eyes to be like other human organizations, what distinguishes the Mystical Body of Christ is that it is sacramental in nature. The mysteries—sacraments revealed by Christ, her founder—bestow salvation and sanctifying grace on its members.

THE CHURCH IS A SACRAMENT

"The Church in this world is the sacrament of salvation, the sign and the instrument of the communion of God and men" (*CCC*, 780). Just as a sacrament of the Church brings us graces and a sharing in the divine life of the Trinity, *the Church itself* is a sacrament among sacraments. Its purpose is to unite human persons to God and to be a source of unity within humanity, drawing together the People of God from every nation.

The Church is the universal sacrament of salvation, in that she is "'the visible plan of God's love for humanity,' because God desires 'that the whole human race may become one People of God, form one Body of Christ, and be built up into the temple of the Holy Spirit'" (*CCC*, 776).

Further, "the Body of Christ" can be thought of in three ways—and all are related to Jesus. Let's look at these three before embarking on the fuller definition of the Mystical Body of Christ.

The first way we refer to the Body of Christ is to talk about the human body that Jesus received in the womb of Mary. The body of Christ, in this first regard, is his flesh and blood, his visage and bodily form.

The second way to talk about the Body of Christ is the Eucharist, or the Body and Blood, soul and divinity, of Jesus. The Eucharist becomes present under the appearances of bread and wine at the Consecration in the Mass. It is what's called the Real Presence of Jesus in the Eucharist. This is a miracle every time it happens! The Church did not make this up; she follows the command of Jesus at the Last Supper: "This is my body, which is given for you. Do this in remembrance of me" (Lk 22:19).

The third way Catholics define the Body of Christ is the mystical kind, otherwise known as the Church. *Mystical* does not mean invisible, for the Church is both visible and invisible, human and divine. The Mystical Body of Christ is definite and able to be perceived by the senses. It is "the unity of the Christian community that is made real."[3]

The "Mystical Body" is not just a clever name for the Church. It relates to Jesus and his communion with us. The Mystical Body of Christ really and truly is God's "divine life . . . dispensed to us through the work of the Holy Spirit."[4]

As Jesus preached about the kingdom of God, he shared an intimate communion with his followers. That communion exists to this very day in Holy Communion. John's gospel offers words from Jesus' own lips describing this mysterious yet real communion between Jesus' body and ours: "Those who eat my flesh and drink my blood abide in me, and I in them. Just as the living Father sent me, and I live because of the Father, so whoever eats me will live because of me" (Jn 6:56–57).

This vivid language, this "eating" as described by Jesus, is literal and really refers to Jesus' sacrifice of his body and blood, present in a nonbloody way. When Jesus first preached these words, some listeners were incredulous (see Jn 6:52, 61–66). To this day, many hearing these words of Jesus receive them with suspicion.

Here's how to receive these words of Jesus by faith.

First, imitate what his closest followers do. Those in the Early Church and the Church today take Jesus at his word. After all, Jesus is "the way, and the truth, and the life" (Jn 14:6). Building on that, St. Cyril of Alexandria says, "Do not doubt whether this is true, but rather receive the words of the Savior in faith, for since he is the truth, he cannot lie" (*CCC*, 1381).

Second, if you desire the Lord Jesus to make his home in you, consider what it means to welcome someone to your home table. You make your guest at home with you by sharing a meal. There is intimate conversation over meals when people truly feel at home. Only in this case, it is Jesus who is inviting you into his presence. He provides the food that we are to eat. And when we agree, we say "Amen," and then we receive him into our interior home, the sanctuary of our souls. Ultimately, this foreshadows the welcome we will receive when we return home to the One who is our true home in heaven.

Never known to mince words, St. Paul is equally blunt as Jesus himself when discussing the truth of the Eucharist. "The cup of blessing that we bless, is it not a sharing in the blood of Christ? The bread that we break, is it not a sharing in the body of Christ? Because there is one bread, we who are many are one body, for we all partake of the one bread" (1 Cor 10:16–17). That's an accurate summary of Jesus' teaching. His Body and Blood is shared that we might have communion with and in him.

With St. Paul's message in mind, Pope Benedict XVI contemplates the impact of the Lord becoming our food.

> Jesus first allowed himself to be opened completely, he has taken us all into himself and has put himself totally into our hands. Hence Communion means the fusion of existences. . . .
>
> The formula "the Church is the Body of Christ" thus states that Eucharist, in which the Lord gives us his body and makes us one body, forever remains the place where the Church is generated, where the Lord himself never ceases to found her anew.[5]

Christ's presence in the Eucharist brings about the "mystical-ness" of the Body of Christ—that is, the Church. It is the fusion of Christ's body with the bodies we have, we who partake of the Eucharist—the Body of the Church.

Jesus describes the necessity of our union, our fusion, our need to abide as one with him. "Abide in me as I abide in you. Just as the branch cannot bear fruit by itself unless it abides in the vine, neither can you unless you abide in me. I am the vine, you are the branches. . . . Apart from me you can do nothing" (Jn 15:4–5).

This is mind-blowing stuff. Let's see where we've been so far. The one true omnipotent God who decides to come to earth—in a human body—uses that same body as a way to save us. On the day he offers up his body to die for us, he also simultaneously and perpetually offers his Body to us as food so we could become part of his Body, the Church. Got that? *Whoa.*

UNITY DESCRIBED THREE WAYS

St. Paul, the great apostle and a leader of the Early Church following Pentecost, was a learned scholar in the Hebrew Scriptures. He's one of the earliest interpreters, or theologians, of Jesus' words regarding "his body, . . . the Church" (Col 1:24). When we read St. Paul, or any New Testament writer, we are going back to the primary sources—to what the Early Church believed and taught after Jesus' resurrection.

St. Paul advances three descriptions of the Church (the Mystical Body of Christ) that still hold relevance for us today. The three ways are "the Bride of Christ," "one Body," and "Christ is the Head of the Body."

First, this idea of Jesus being the Bridegroom and the Church being his Bride is something we've seen before, but let's quickly recap using the words of St. Paul.

St. Paul likens the act of love, the one-flesh union between a husband and a wife, to the life of Jesus and the Church, Bridegroom and Bride, when he says, "'A man will leave his father and mother and be joined to his wife, and the two will become one flesh.' This is a great mystery, and I am applying it to Christ and the church" (Eph 5:31–32). (See Eph 5:22–32 for the whole passage.)

In human terms, a marriage is an intimate relationship, and when conditions are right, it is capable of bringing new life into the world. Thinking in spiritual terms, the love of Christ for his Church is always begetting spiritual children, born to Mother Church through Baptism, and nurtured by her teachings and sacraments.

Paul's nuptial references were right on the mark, building on well-known themes dating back to the prophets. Church teaching leans heavily on Paul's letters.

> The theme of Christ as Bridegroom of the Church was prepared for by the prophets and announced by John the Baptist [see Jn 3:29]. The Lord referred to himself as the "bridegroom" [Mk 2:19]. The Apostle speaks of the whole Church and of each of the faithful, members of his Body, as a bride "betrothed" to Christ the Lord so as to become but one spirit with him [cf. Mt 22:1–14, 25:1–13; 1 Cor 6:15–17; 2 Cor 11:2]. The Church is the spotless bride of the spotless Lamb. "Christ loved the Church and gave himself up for her, that he might sanctify her" [Eph 5:25–26]. He has joined her with himself in an everlasting covenant and never stops caring for her as for his own body. (CCC, 796)

A second way St. Paul offers wisdom on the union between Christ and his Church is that she is "one Body." The Church gathers around Christ and in him via Baptism and the Eucharist.

> In the one Spirit we were all baptized into one body—Jews or Greeks, slaves or free—and we were all made to drink of one Spirit.
> Indeed, the body does not consist of one member but of many. If the foot would say, "Because I am not a hand, I do not belong to the body," that would not make it any less a part of the body. And if the ear would say, "Because I am not an eye, I do not belong to the body," that would not make it any less a part of the body. If the whole body were an eye, where would the hearing be? If the whole body were hearing, where would the sense of smell be? But as it is, God arranged the members in the body, each one of

them, as he chose. If all were a single member, where would the body be? As it is, there are many members, yet one body. The eye cannot say to the hand, "I have no need of you," nor again the head to the feet, "I have no need of you." On the contrary, the members of the body that seem to be weaker are indispensable. . . . If one member suffers, all suffer together with it; if one member is honored, all rejoice together with it. (1 Cor 12:12–22, 26)

In a world prizing individuality and separateness, the Church offers a common unity among its believers despite their diverse gifts. Even though the Church is one body, it "does not do away with the diversity of its members" (CCC, 791).

With a view toward the Eucharist, the Early Church taught respect toward the different members of the Church, likening them to the grains of wheat that come together to make a loaf of bread. Pope Pius XII captured this lovely image in his encyclical on the Mystical Body of Christ and shows how this holy food fills us with supernatural charity. "The Sacrament of the Eucharist is itself a striking and wonderful figure of the unity of the Church, if we consider how in the bread to be consecrated many grains go to form one whole . . . and that in it the very Author of supernatural grace is given to us, so that through Him we may receive the spirit of charity in which we are bidden to live now no longer our own life but the life of Christ, and to love the Redeemer Himself in all the members of His . . . Body."[6]

What moves me about Pius XII's words here is that they were written during the darkest years of World War II, when humanity's very soul was threatened to be lost to the carnage of war between so many nations. Pope Pius XII's words begged for an increased fervor among Christians in their affinity with and belonging to the Mystical Body of

Christ—as a cause for hope for the salvation of the world. We need to take notes on living this out today.

The *Catechism* teaches that "the unity of the Mystical Body triumphs over all human divisions" (*CCC*, 791). That is why I could say, in chapter 1, that my belonging to the Church was greater than my family history, medical history, work history, and so on. My identity is rooted in Christ first and in being a child of God. But that's just speaking for myself, personally. The Mystical Body of Christ has global implications in leading us toward charity toward our neighbors—and especially our enemies. "You are all children of God through faith. As many of you as were baptized into Christ have clothed yourselves with Christ. There is no longer Jew or Greek, there is no longer slave or free, there is no longer male and female; for all of you are one in Christ Jesus" (Gal 3:26–28).

The Mystical Body of Christ is God's plan for love in the world. St. Joan of Arc, who suffered for the faith and died by being burned at the stake, sums it up: "About Jesus Christ and the Church, I simply know they're just one thing, and we shouldn't complicate the matter" (*CCC*, 795).

The third important thought from St. Paul regarding the Mystical Body is that, though there are many members, Jesus Christ is always the Head of the Body.

St. Paul's Letter to the Colossians captures the majesty of Jesus' primacy: "He is the image of the invisible God, the firstborn of all creation; for in him all things in heaven and on earth were created, things visible and invisible, whether thrones or dominions or rulers or powers—all things have been created through him and for him. He himself is before all things, and in him all things hold together. He is the head of the body, the church; he is the beginning, the firstborn from the dead, so that he might come to have first place in everything" (Col 1:15–18). Staying united to Christ—and the Church—is our positive response to God's love.

If you are not squeamish, think of it this way: a body without a head is a corpse. That image is a very grievous thing, taken in the literal sense. But for the life of the Spirit, that same image says much about how vital our personal connection with Christ is, not to mention how important is the integrity with which our churches operate for "in him all things hold together" (Col 1:17).

We must always look to stay in union with the Head of the Church, our Divine Friend, Savior, and King, Jesus. Without him, we can do nothing.[7] From a Christian standpoint, separation from God is deadly.

St. Thomas Aquinas taught, "Head and members form as it were one and the same mystical person" (*CCC*, 795). So when it comes Christ and the Church, and our part in the Mystical Body, I try to stay within that merciful caution we've talked about: what God has joined, we must not divide.

Confidence in the Mystical Body of Christ is a matter of trust in what Jesus and the members of his Church have taught and written about it, especially those who have died for it—saints like St. Paul and St. Joan of Arc. The martyrs died to bring this faith to me.

I have confidence in the Mystical Body of Christ because Jesus has already proved to me how committed he is to defending his Bride. Jesus is all in for the Church. He gives up everything he has for her sake, including his own blood. Plus, my life is enriched by the Church's graces, which help me live a life of following Jesus the Beloved, my Divine Friend.

I trust that the Mystical Body of Christ is part of God's plan to unite us to Christ and his Church and to win the entire world to Christ.

We can have confidence in the Church because it *is* the Mystical Body of Christ!

Next time you're in a Catholic church, light a candle for your intentions. It's not a shot in the dark; it's faith in the light who is Christ and in the saintly members of the Mystical Body already in glory.

PRAY

Meditate on the Body of Christ as described by St. Paul in 1 Corinthians 12.

LEARN

Read *Mystici Corporis Christi* by Pope Pius XII, found at the Vatican website: http://w2.vatican.va/content/pius-xii/en/encyclicals/documents/hf_p-xii_enc_29061943_mystici-corporis-christi.html.

ENGAGE

Find out when Easter Sunday is then make plans to attend the Easter Vigil the evening before.

CHAPTER 8

LOVE OF NEIGHBOR

THE POWER OF "AS"

No way! That's pretty much what I thought when I heard that two years after being shot, Pope John Paul II would visit his would-be assassin, Mehmet Ali Ağca, in prison. Reports said John Paul II had sincerely forgiven his assailant in that meeting.

The pope also asked Italy's president to pardon Ağca, which eventually happened in 2000. Ağca was then sent back to his native country, Turkey, where he was promptly arrested in connection to other crimes. He served time until 2010.

During the Christmas season of 2014, Mehmet Ali Ağca returned to St. Peter's Basilica as a free man, laying roses at John Paul II's tomb. I don't pretend to know what was in Ağca's heart; there are many conflicting reports about his life after prison.

None of that changes the point that it was widely reported that John Paul II outright forgave Ağca during that prison visit and stayed in touch with the man and his family over the years.

It's hard for most of us to fathom creating a connection like that. We could almost rationalize the forgiveness part from a healthy-living standpoint. It was a way for the pope to heal and move on. For any victim, a key component in recovery and healing from hurts, especially those wounds caused from violence, is the forgiveness of one's assailant either in person or from a safe distance. From where I sit, John Paul II never once acted like a victim but rather as a healer.

St. John Paul II showed us how to deal with the injunction from Jesus in the Lord's Prayer: "to forgive us our trespasses, *as* we forgive those who trespass against us." That little word *as* tells me that if I really want to understand forgiveness and mercy, I need to learn it from the inside out. I need to extend forgiveness and mercy even when nobody has asked me for it—even if their contrition and apology is never forthcoming. I am to lead with mercy even when it feels counterintuitive.

As the photos of those two men in the jail cell—the pontiff and the criminal—circulated in the press, the world witnessed the power of God's love and grace in action.

John Paul II is a saint for many reasons, but forgiving a person who tried to kill him in cold blood? That's the one that stands out for me. That's as powerful as *as* gets—to forgive *as* Jesus did. From the Cross, Jesus prayed for his executioners, "Father, forgive them" (Lk 23:34). Jesus and his good friend, John Paul II, both demonstrate bold confidence in mercy, and such confidence is born of prayer.

So this is why belonging to the Church matters—that we might have a robust prayer life that empowers our love of our neighbor. Prayer changes us because we begin to live in tune with the Holy Spirit's leadings and promptings. Prayer is leaning on the chest of Jesus, like the beloved disciple did at the Last Supper. We desire to be close enough to Jesus to hear his heartbeat—and to let him know ours!

Think back to where we've come from in this book.

So much of what we have talked about has centered on the Incarnation and Jesus becoming a man, taking on real human flesh and the experiences of humanity. That means we have a God who *gets* us! He's a God who knows our weaknesses and those times that we think loving others is impossible!

Jesus' time on earth was to show us the best way to be human! And the best way to be a human is to love, and the best way to learn to love is to spend time with the Lord of love, Jesus, in prayer. In prayer, God's life begins to take flesh in us. Who we love—God—becomes incarnate in us.

Most times, it's easy to love our friends and family— it's easy to love the ones who love us in return, so I'm not going to spend time on that. You might even be able to do that without much prayer—just the strength of your relationship with the other person facilitates that love. I'm not recommending you live without prayer, of course.

The real grist for this chapter is loving our neighbor when it is hard, or when we are at odds with the other, or when we are facing an enemy. These are exactly the times we need to focus on the big *as*—we can only love this way by imitating how Jesus has loved us. And we will know how only by prayer—in heart-to-heart conversation with Christ.

Most of the world is familiar with the command from Jesus that we are to "love one another." But we learn the depth of that love when we pay attention to the second half of that phrase from Jesus: "as I have loved you." Again the *as*! "This is my commandment, that you love one another as I have loved you" (Jn 15:12).

This is a summary of the mission of the Mystical Body of Christ. All who belong to the Church are charged with this important call to love. Thus we see how the now-sainted John Paul II, whom we are assured is a beloved son of God and friend of Jesus, ventured into a conversation of forgiveness with the convict who tried to assassinate him.

TRUSTING THE DIVINE MERCY

It comes as no surprise that John Paul II brought increased devotion to Jesus' title as Divine Mercy to the Church. He was already living mercy's message in his own life. John Paul II even added a feast day to the liturgical calendar. The first Sunday after Easter is "Divine Mercy Sunday."

The devotion to Divine Mercy[1] started in John Paul II's native Poland through the mission Jesus endowed to a humble nun, Sr. Maria Faustina Kowalska. She was later named a saint by the pontiff in 2000.[2] The centerpiece of this devotion is the trust that souls place in the mercy of Jesus. To trust in Divine Mercy is to know that no soul, while living on earth, is beyond God's mercy. Mercy is a free gift to those who ask! What's more, we can ask God's help so that we too might become more merciful.

One of the simplest and most powerful prayers to invoke to Divine Mercy is "Jesus, I trust in you!"

What a confidence booster! "Jesus, I trust in you!" applies to so many situations! And how simple to repeat it over and over again like a child, whenever we need it. We are children of God, and we've got to grow in confidence when asking for what we need. "Jesus, I trust in you!" is both a proclamation and petition of our confidence in God's presence and control of life's events.

This short, heroic prayer of trust in Jesus is much like Mary's fiat: "Let it be . . . according to your word" (Lk 1:38). Both are prayers we can pray daily. Both are prayers of surrender to follow God's way, not ours. Both engage great hope that God has got a better plan than we do.

Mary's fiat and "Jesus, I trust in you!" open our hearts to love! When we give Jesus our fiat and our trust, it is like praying, "I'm putting you first, Lord; I want to follow your lead."

This is entrustment! It's where the power to love comes from—by trusting in God, not in ourselves. That's how we learn to love when we are in difficult situations or with difficult people. We let mercy lead—not our judgments, not our measured responses, not the woulda-coulda-shouldas, and not the fear that our love is not enough. God's powerful mercy and love banishes our limitations.

Do not forget: God is love. God loved us first. God initiates love. He does not wait for us to come to him. He comes in search of us! He does not force his love but offers his love and respects our human freedom to accept or reject him. Whatever difficult situations that we face in loving and caring for others, when we let Jesus take the lead, we are in a position of inviting Jesus' presence into those human connections. We must let him help us initiate the loving actions that need to be taken.

Jesus said, "Love one another as I have loved you" (see Jn 13:34). That's hard enough on most days, even when we love the person in question. Jesus is calling us to an all-in kind of love—to love our neighbor, even when it is difficult, and more plainly, to love our enemies.

Jesus' commission to the children of God is this:

> You have heard that it was said, "You shall love your neighbor and hate your enemy." But I say to you, Love your enemies and pray for those who persecute you, so that you may be children of your Father in heaven; for he makes his sun rise on the evil and on the good, and sends rain on the righteous and on the unrighteous. For if you love those who love you, what reward do you have? Do not even the tax collectors do the same? And if you greet only your brothers and sisters, what more are you doing than others? Do not even the Gentiles do the same? Be perfect, therefore, as your heavenly Father is perfect. (Mt 5:43–48)

"INCREASE YOUR MERCY IN US"

One of my favorite prayers related to the Divine Mercy devotion comes from the diary[3] belonging to St. Maria Faustina. When I pray the Divine Mercy Chaplet,[4] and I conclude it with this short prayer, I am reminded that mercy is the will of God both for me and for *all* the people I encounter in my life—as well as for *all* the world.

> Eternal God, in whom mercy is endless
> and the treasury of compassion inexhaustible,
> look kindly upon us and increase your mercy in us,
> that in difficult moments we might not despair
> nor become despondent,
> but with great confidence
> submit ourselves to your holy will,
> which is Love and Mercy itself.
> Amen.

God's will for us begins and ends with his love and mercy. The measure of mercy that we have received is the starting point for the mercy and love we are to give to others.

The short but potent prayer above reminds our hearts of the depth of God's love for us—it is a deep, deep well that we may draw upon with confident assurance. More than that, the prayer asks God to "increase [his] mercy in us." That is a prayer that delights God, one that he will always answer. He is waiting for us to take the chance to be more like him. We can pray, "Increase your mercy in us, Lord!" And God says, "Of course I will! I've been waiting for you to ask—to give me permission to act in you—to help you love others as I have loved you."

Prayer is our encounter with Jesus, a living relationship that transforms us. Prayer helps to move us out of selfishness and into trust. In prayer we put ourselves into God's hands. When we trust Jesus in prayer, we trust him to work out his will in our lives in a merciful way because his very will "is Love and Mercy itself."

The holy ones, the saints and future saints, know we need prayer in order to love without blocks or limits. Madeleine Delbrêl, a twentieth-century atheist who converted to Catholicism, wrote about prayer being key to genuine love.

> Faith and hope are given to us in prayer. So, without prayer, we will not be able to love. It is in prayer and only in prayer that the Christ who is in each person is revealed to us through a faith that becomes increasingly more sharply focused and more clear-sighted. It is in prayer that we can ask for those gifts for each person without which there is no genuine love; it is through prayer that our hope grows so we may cope with the number of people that we meet and the depth of their needs.
>
> It is our faith and hope growing through prayer that removes the obstacle that most blocks the road of love: namely a concern for ourselves. It is not our love that we have to offer; it is the love of God.[5]

Is God asking for the impossible when it comes to loving others and loving even our enemies? St. John Paul II became friendly with the man who intentionally tried to kill him. If I see this feat through my own feelings and not through the eyes of faith, it seems impossible. If we do not separate the power of faith and hope from our love, it becomes possible. Faith and hope increase mercy in us. This is the power of love Jesus desires us to have, to help change the world.

Pope Benedict XVI's encyclical *Deus Caritas Est* teaches that when we know the love of the Divine Friend—Jesus—first in prayer, we can love boldly:

Love of neighbor is thus shown to be possible in the way proclaimed by the Bible, by Jesus. It consists in the very fact that, in God and with God, I love even the person whom I do not like or even know. This can only take place on the basis of an intimate encounter with God, an encounter which has become a communion of will, even affecting my feelings. Then I learn to look on this other person not simply with my eyes and my feelings, but from the perspective of Jesus Christ. His friend is my friend. . . .

Only if I serve my neighbor can my eyes be opened to what God does for me and how much he loves me. The saints—consider the example of [St.] Teresa of Calcutta—constantly renewed their capacity for love of neighbor from their encounter with the Eucharistic Lord, and conversely this encounter acquired its realism and depth in their service to others. Love of God and love of neighbor are thus inseparable, they form a single commandment. But both live from the love of God who has loved us first.[6]

THE REAL STAIRWAY TO HEAVEN

You'd think a name like Fulgentius would be hard to forget. I don't think I've ever pronounced his name the same way twice. But his sermon about two well-known martyrs, one responsible for the murder of the other, is forever etched in my mind. St. Fulgentius of Ruspe, a fifth-century bishop in North Africa, offers a riveting sermon that is part of the Liturgy of the Hours for the day after Christmas, December 26, the Feast of St. Stephen.

Stephen was an early martyr whose stoning is recorded in the Acts of the Apostles. Acts describes Stephen, one of the first deacons, as "a man full of faith and the Holy Spirit . . . full of grace and power" (Acts 6:5, 8). It was said that "his face was like the face of an angel" (Acts 6:15). He was arrested for being a disciple of Jesus, but he continued preaching the Gospel while under arrest, right up until his violent death by stoning.

St. Fulgentius's sermon, on the day after Christmas, begins by describing the birth of the Savior Jesus and the death of the martyr Stephen.

> Yesterday we celebrated the birth in time of the eternal king. Today we celebrate the triumphant suffering of his soldier. Yesterday our king, clothed in his robe of flesh, left his place in the virgin's womb and graciously visited the world. Today his soldier leaves the tabernacle of his body and goes triumphantly to heaven. . . .
>
> And so the love that brought Christ from heaven to earth raised Stephen from earth to heaven; shown first in the king, it later shone forth in the soldier. Love was Stephen's weapon by which he gained every battle, and so won the crown signified by his name. His love of God kept him from yielding to the ferocious mob; his love for his neighbor made him pray for those who were stoning him. Love inspired him to reprove those who erred, to make them amend; love led him to pray for those who stoned him, to save them from punishment.[7]

Just as Jesus prayed "Father, forgive them" (Lk 23:34) for those who crucified him, Stephen prays aloud for his enemies even while being put to death by their stoning him. Then Stephen experiences a vision of heaven before he dies a martyr's death:

> Filled with the Holy Spirit, he gazed into heaven and saw the glory of God and Jesus standing at the right hand of God. "Look," he said, "I see the heavens opened and the Son of Man standing at the right hand of God!" But they covered their ears, and with a loud shout all rushed together against him. Then

they dragged him out of the city and began to stone him; and the witnesses laid their coats at the feet of a young man named Saul. While they were stoning Stephen, he prayed, "Lord Jesus, receive my spirit." Then he knelt down and cried out in a loud voice, "Lord, do not hold this sin against them." When he had said this, he died. (Acts 7:55–60)

One additional, important note: the young man, Saul, overseeing the stoning and approving of Stephen's death would later have a profound conversion recorded in Acts 9. Saul would become the great apostle Paul who is quoted liberally in this book. Stephen's desire was to win Saul's soul for Christ.

Back to the sermon from Fulgentius: "Strengthened by the power of his love, [Stephen] overcame the raging cruelty of Saul and won his persecutor on earth as his companion in heaven. In his long and tireless love he longed to gain by prayer those whom he could not convert by admonition."[8]

My favorite part of this sermon is when Fulgentius takes the long view—all the way to when both saints are no longer enemies but *friends in heaven*!

Now at last, Paul rejoices with Stephen, with Stephen he delights in the glory of Christ, with Stephen he exults, with Stephen he reigns. Stephen went first, slain by the stones of Paul, but Paul followed after, helped by the prayer of Stephen. This surely, is the true life . . . a life where Paul feels no shame because of Stephen's death, and Stephen delights in Paul's companionship, for love fills them both with joy. It was Stephen's love that prevailed over the cruelty of the mob, and it was Paul's love that covered a multitude of his sins; and it was love that won for both of them the kingdom of heaven.[9]

The first time I absorbed this text I wept. The truth is that both men are now side by side in heaven. If anyone had the right to hold a grudge, it was Stephen, whose death was at the hands of Saul, the future Paul, and the mob. Yet Stephen, even in death, wanted nothing more but to convert Saul and his cohort for the love of God. Stephen's love for his enemies makes Paul's future conversion all the sweeter.

"It was love that won for both of them the kingdom of heaven." This inspiring depiction of Stephen and Paul's joy is the truth of the matter. Each man came to love Jesus Christ at a different time, and yet the order does not matter! Stephen welcomes the sight of Paul, his persecutor, into his heavenly purview. He longed to gain by his prayers those he could not convince with his preaching on earth—including Paul.

I think of all the difficult people I have known—who will likely be in heaven—as well as all the friends and loved ones who are no longer a part of this life of mine, and I'm both shamed and consoled. Our persecutors on earth may be, one day, our companions in heaven! Yet I can still hope to gain perhaps, by my fervent prayers today, those future companions I may have lost by my neglect or ignorance or lack of charity.

Lord have mercy on all the "deaths" I have witnessed, and all the times I have smugly thought that I was right and not in the wrong. How many "Stephens" have been stoned to death while I watched? Can I be redeemed? Yes. Can I be forgiven? Yes. Can I one day be in heaven—sharing the love and the joy of those I've hurt? Yes, with God's grace, yes. Yes.

St. Fulgentius closes his sermon with a vote of confidence in the power of love of neighbor: it is the stairway to heaven. Love of neighbor, and in particular the love of enemies or difficult neighbors, is the stair-climb of saints such as Stephen, Paul, Faustina, and John Paul II. It's the

spiritual muscle-building and holy cardio that you and I
need.

> Love, indeed, is the source of all good things; it is
> an impregnable defense, and the way that leads to
> heaven. He who walks in love can neither go astray
> nor be afraid: love guides him, protects him, and
> brings him to his journey's end. . . .
>   Christ made love the stairway that would enable
> all Christians to climb to heaven. Hold fast to it,
> therefore, in all sincerity, give one another practical
> proof of it, and by your progress in it, make your
> ascent together.[10]

Love of our enemies is possible only by first allowing Jesus
to conquer the enemies of love within ourselves.

We may look at the darkness and selfishness in our
hearts and say, *no way!* Then let us hold fast to mercy and
pray:

> Lord, increase your mercy in us!
> That in difficult moments we might not despair
> nor become despondent,
> but with great confidence
> submit ourselves to your holy will
> which is Love and Mercy itself.
> Amen.

PRAY

Choose one of these scriptures to meditate on:
- Jesus' preaching on the Good Samaritan in Luke
  10:25–37.
- St. Paul's preaching on love in 1 Corinthians 13:1–13.

LEARN

The *Catechism* offers in-depth commentary on the Ten
Commandments. More than 350 paragraphs are dedicated
to this great theme, the love of neighbor, from 2197 to 2557.

The *Catechism* is designed with brief summaries following each major article. For an overview of this subject, read the following summaries:

The fourth commandment: 2247–2257
The fifth commandment: 2318–2330
The sixth commandment: 2392–2400
The seventh commandment: 2450–2463
The eighth commandment: 2504–2513
The ninth commandment: 2528–2533
The tenth commandment: 2551–2557

ENGAGE

Discover the Chaplet of Divine Mercy, or the Novena to Divine Mercy, as suggested by St. John Paul II and St. Maria Faustina Kowalska. The last three popes have preached widely on this theme of mercy. And this book has been written, largely, during the Jubilee Year of Mercy announced by Pope Francis.

The Marians of the Immaculate Conception play a strong role in educating Catholics and others about the necessity of knowing God's mercy in our lives and spreading it through love of neighbor. For prayers, articles, and videos on this subject, go to http://www.thedivinemercy.org.

THE DIGNITY OF THE HUMAN PERSON

FOR HEAVEN'S SAKE

I don't know about you, but when I became a parent my perspective on the world changed. I developed a greater awareness of the beauty and goodness of life—especially how the wonder of God's handiwork and creation was immediately evident to me whenever I looked into the eyes of my little ones. At other moments I also saw, with new intensity, the darkness of the world right outside the door of our home. Once I became responsible for another little human life, it was as if I had grown an invisible antenna picking up signals 24/7 of all things safe and unsafe for my children.

Before I became a parent, I was never too strict about what I ate or drank. I lived with an appreciation of "all things in moderation" and went on my merry way. Once I became pregnant, suddenly I reconsidered eating and drinking. One of many dietary changes during pregnancy was fasting from my favorite wines and alcoholic beverages to safeguard my growing baby *in utero*.

Before I became a parent, I'd hear about tragic news events and offer prayers for those in harm's way. And then, more or less, I went on my merry way. After becoming a parent, between the twenty-four-hour news cycle of the broadcast and cable networks and the incessant drone from websites and social media, I became ever more aware of the sacredness of human life. I also became more vigilant in safeguarding it, for my family's sake, from threats caused by economic, political, religious, and social unrest.

Early in my parenting years I encountered the true hope of heaven. Before I was a parent, heaven was out there somewhere in perhaps the distant future; the existence of such a state was a matter of faith. After I became diagnosed with breast cancer as a parent of young children, the truth of heaven's meaning became more real for me.

Heaven was no longer some place I needed to prepare for some distant someday. As I dealt with the limitations of my mortality, it took on new immediacy. Heaven would be the home where I would hope to be reunited with my family forever. This was most consoling on my worst days after diagnosis, for I feared if my disease progressed too fast, I would miss my little ones growing up. Heaven became my very real hope, based on Jesus' words and the faith professed by the Catholic Church.

It's been more than twenty years since that worrisome diagnosis, and heaven is still my hope. It helps me to view each day with an eternal perspective. I've come to know that *all* human life is priceless, regardless of how many days one spends on earth.

Our true destiny is to live with God and our sisters and brothers in the kingdom forever.

BLESSED BY THE FATHER

The Father's plan is to unite all humanity into one family, the Church. Our baptisms confer that dignity on us. And that brings me to the confidence I have in the Church as "the sign and safeguard of the transcendent dimension of the human person."[1]

I'm all in when it comes to the Catholic Church not just because it preaches heaven but because it holds sacred *all* human persons. It is the only institution on earth with a heavenly perspective on how awesome every single person is created to be. We are created with human freedom, so we, in a certain sense, will choose heaven for ourselves based on how closely we follow the ways of the kingdom of God.

Jesus will one day come as King, and we ought to be ready. In the gospels Jesus preaches about his Second Coming and the final judgment that will take place at the end of time. He will arrive in his glory, with all his angels with him, and will be seated on a glorious throne. From there Jesus will separate all the peoples like a shepherd separates sheep and goats. Those who have followed Jesus and his ways will be invited to his heavenly kingdom, where they will be the delight of their Father forever.

> Then the king will say to those at his right hand, "Come, you that are blessed by my Father, inherit the kingdom prepared for you from the foundation of the world; for I was hungry and you gave me food, I was thirsty and you gave me something to drink, I was a stranger and you welcomed me, I was naked and you gave me clothing, I was sick and you took care of me, I was in prison and you visited me. . . . Truly I tell you, just as you did it to one of the least of these who are members of my family, you did it to me." (Mt 25:34–36, 40)

We hear the blessed dignity that Jesus affords to his family and the truth of our destiny if we follow him: "Come, you that are blessed by my father." That's what our baptisms made us—beloved children who will inherit what our Father bequeaths to us.

To be blessed by our Father is our future glory! It should direct our lives! Our Father in heaven awaits total union with his children in glory. That future dignity and future unity begins here on earth in the dignity we have as sons and daughters of God.

Finally, those same verses from Matthew's gospel regarding the Second Coming of Christ show us how Jesus personally identifies himself—"you did it to me"—with all our actions, or inactions, toward others. If we give someone a drink, we are serving Jesus. If take care of someone who is sick, we are serving Jesus. We're not serving Jesus just because we're doing good; we are actually serving the Jesus that resides in that person. This is the powerful connection of Jesus to the Mystical Body. What we do for others, we do for Jesus. How we treat the dignity and the needs of our brothers and sisters matters to him.

Another aspect of our being blessed by our Father in heaven is the transformation we will experience in what the Apostles' Creed calls the resurrection of the body. We will no longer have earthbound bodies but heavenly ones. That means each of us will be reunited with the body we had before death, but it will be a glorified body, not just a recycled one. To a cancer survivor like me, this is really good news. Our glorified bodies will be without disease, wrinkles, or decay. They will reflect our best selves. Our old earthly bodies will have perished, and our transcendent selves will live no longer bound to the perils of mortality. We will dwell in a heavenly body for eternity.

The Church's vision of the human person is linked with eternity. That's because the Church is the seed and the beginning of the kingdom of God, which will last forever. Our faith is the beginning of eternal life. From their baptisms until their natural deaths, Christians are called to ongoing renewal and transformation while keeping their eyes fixed on heaven.

We are made for heaven. It is important to keep that in mind when the world closes in on us, when we feel dragged down by it, or on a day when we feel small and insignificant. We are not random specks floating detached in an impersonal universe. We are made to know the infinite God as a Father, and we are made to live to infinity. That's not insignificant!

I always smile when I think about the cartoon figure Buzz Lightyear from the Toy Story movie series. Buzz helps his friends to have hope and to think big—the way God thinks of us—when he declares, "To infinity and beyond!" For Christians with the hope of heaven, that's not wishful thinking or a catchy phrase from a movie script—that's a pretty accurate description of eternal life!

In heaven, we'll know the other side of infinity. For we will know a love that never ends and we will be known by the one who made us and knows us the best. We will know the Blessed Trinity and ourselves in blessed perfection. We will be fully initiated into the Communion of Saints that we profess as Catholics.

I've always admired how the very first line of the prologue of the *Catechism of the Catholic Church* offers Jesus' words as a blueprint not only for the purpose of the *Catechism* but for our life's goal to know God intimately. Quoting Jesus' prayer for us, John's gospel reads: "Father . . . this is eternal life, that they may know you, the only true God, and Jesus Christ whom you have sent" (Jn 17:13).

Jesus' coming was to offer us a share in the divine life. The Church safeguards this extraordinary vision of the human person. And the saints of the Church Triumphant exhort us to live, as they have, from this hope in our identity and from the belief in the life to come.

The saints always get it right. The saints of the Church are more spectacular and beautiful than the stars and galaxies of the cosmos, which will eventually burn out. But a saint will never burn out or fade away. Their lives shine with the perpetual light of Christ. That's why I love to quote the saints as we consider our own pilgrim journey to heaven.

St. Paul's famous ode to love in 1 Corinthians 13 ends with this understanding of the eternal love reserved for us in heaven, where we will be known better than we have been known before by any human person: "Love never ends. But as for prophecies, they will come to an end; as for tongues, they will cease; as for knowledge, it will come to an end. For we know only in part, and we prophesy only in part; but when the complete comes, the partial will come to an end. . . . For now we see in a mirror, dimly, but then we will see face to face. Now I know only in part; then I will know fully, even as I have been fully known" (1 Cor 13:8–10, 12).

Heaven ought to be the goal animating all our pursuits. It's a holy struggle, but we are worthy of undertaking it so that we may arrive at this eternal love that will make us utterly happy. Thank God for holy saints—and their pep talks that encourage us to strive after heaven!

St. Robert Bellarmine, a sixteenth-century bishop, offers powerful advice: "If you are wise, then, know that you have been created for the glory of God and your own eternal salvation. This is your goal; this is the center of your life; this is the treasure of your heart. If you reach this goal, you will find happiness. If you fail to reach it, you will find misery."[2]

Our route to heaven is not a solo project. It's communal, and our communion with others plays a vital role in whether we'll be akin to sheep or goats in the final judgment. And so we'll turn now to exploring how the dignity of the human person, and our treatment of others, is the key to all of Catholic social thought and practice and how it offers us a call to action to love one another in many dynamic ways.

THE HIGHEST MOUNTAIN, THE HIGHEST PRINCIPLE

God the Father has invested great faith in us as human beings by sending Jesus to earth to secure our salvation and by offering life everlasting. Like a good mother, the Catholic Church wants to make us saints—to nurture the divine life in us and to bring us one day to meet our Father in heaven, to see him face-to-face.

The Church has such a high opinion of human persons—because God does! And that is why *the dignity of the human person* is the cornerstone of all Catholic social teaching.

If we lined up all the major points of Catholic social teaching and compared them, by analogy, to the Himalayas, *the dignity of the human person* would be Mount Everest—the most magnificent and tallest peak, dwarfing the rest. All other social teachings fall under the shadow cast by the dignity of the human person. Not only that, but all other social actions gain their legitimacy from how well they affirm the dignity of the human person.

There are two major reasons why this is true.

But first, here's a brain-teasing riddle from catechism class that will help us uncover the reason: What are the only *man-made* things in heaven? Take your time. Puzzle it out. We can wait . . .

Answer: the nail prints on the hands and feet of Jesus and the scar in his side.

Jesus' body maintains these scars as proof of his resurrection to the scoffers who could not believe he was the one who was crucified and died and was buried.

It's amazing to consider that Jesus *still* has a human body. The New Testament backs this up, describing the risen Lord. Most famously, Jesus appeared to Thomas and the apostles, inviting Thomas to probe the scar and nail prints to assuage his doubt (see Jn 20:24–29).

Just consider this for a moment. Right now, the omnipotent, omniscient, omnipresent, almighty Savior of the world still has a human body, albeit a glorified one. The post-Resurrection accounts verify its amazing properties: walking through walls and startling appearances and disappearances (see Lk 24:31, 36–43; Jn 20:19–20).

So the reason why the dignity of the human person is so important is answered by the Incarnation of Jesus— "The Word became flesh" (Jn 1:14). "The Church thus confesses that Jesus is inseparably true God and true man. He is truly the Son of God who, without ceasing to be God and Lord, became a man and our brother. . . . 'The Son of God . . . worked with human hands; he thought with a human mind. He acted with a human will, and with a human heart he loved. Born of the Virgin Mary, he has truly been made one of us, like to us in all things except sin'" (CCC, 469–470). The body of Jesus was not some kind of disposable earthly transport vehicle. No. Jesus completely united himself to humanity in a permanent way.

The humanity of Jesus signals to us the deep meaning of the human person. All human persons are honored by Jesus' choice to cloak his divinity with human skin. The most powerful sign of our dignity is that Jesus, God himself, took on a body. "Christ by his Incarnation has united himself in some fashion with every person."[3]

However, even before Jesus came to earth, the primacy of the dignity of the human person is found within the first few pages of the Bible, in the creation of man and woman.

> Then God said, "Let us make humankind in our image, according to our likeness; and let them have dominion over . . . the earth."
> So God created humankind in his image,
>   in the image of God he created them;
>   male and female he created them. (Gn 1:26–27)

The first creation account declares man and woman were made in the *image* and *likeness* of God! This is another reason why human dignity is the primordial foundation to all social teachings. The *Catechism of the Catholic Church* summarizes it this way: "The dignity of the human person is rooted in his creation in the image and likeness of God" (CCC, 1700).

Humanity being made in the image and likeness of God and God becoming man are intrinsic to God's plan. These inner truths unlock the richness of Catholic social teaching. All other teachings flow out and radiate from these core values.

Great saints such as St. Teresa of Calcutta reminded us to see Jesus in the face of another person, especially if he wore the "distressing disguise" of the poorest of the poor. Jesus is the face behind the least, the lonely, the lost, and the littlest ones. Mother Teresa, as she was known to millions, taught that if you find Jesus in the hiddenness of the host in the Eucharist, you could find Jesus in another person.

My favorite quotation from the *Compendium of the Social Doctrine of the Church* is this, and it is worth memorizing: "Since something of the glory of God shines on the face of every person, the dignity of every person before God is the basis of the dignity of man before other men."[4]

Something of the glory of God shines on your face. The next time you're having a bad day, consider that.

My favorite musical of all time captures this very idea. Love of God and the dignity we must afford our neighbors is a theme that has captivated millions of theatergoers who've experienced the Broadway musical *Les Misérables*. Based on Victor Hugo's novel, the musical offers a breathtaking moment in its finale. While most of the audience clutches Kleenex, the company sings in full voice, "To love another person is to see the face of God." Truth.

To Change the World

Everything we've covered about the dignity of the human person lays the groundwork for how the Church and world ought to be engaged in an ongoing dialogue for the hope of a better world. The transformation that comes from renewal in the life of a Christian, and within the family of God, ought to lead to the transformation of society—a holy ripple effect.

The Church's teaching on the dignity of the human person is a guide for the moral consciences of individuals, local communities, and nations, be they members of the Church or not. The Church is a light to the world not only in her teachings but better still when her members live a devoted life of faith in view of their neighbors. "Thus the Church, at once 'a visible association and a spiritual community,' goes forward together with humanity and experiences the same earthly lot which the world does. She serves as a leaven and as a kind of soul for human society as it is to be renewed in Christ and transformed into God's family."[5]

Catholic social doctrine has many important principles, such as the common good, the universal distribution of goods (under which one finds the preferential option for the poor), participation, subsidiarity, and solidarity. The dignity of the human person is foundational to all of them. While we will not make those principles our study here, it is important to understand that one can draw lines that connect human dignity to how each of those principles operates in society.

There are many intersections between upholding the dignity of human persons and the pressing social issues of our day, and we'll take a moment to describe a few.

Understanding the dignity of the human person is particularly relevant for human life issues. The Church never wavers in her respect for the life of the body and care for the dignity of the human person in every circumstance of natural life, for the body is also a *temple* of the Holy Spirit (see 1 Cor 3:16). This explains why the Church has always stood for marriage and family life and against contraception and abortion in all its forms. And it's why caring for the elderly and the sick and infirm must override any calls for doctor-assisted suicide or euthanasia of any kind.

Understanding the dignity of the human person plays a role in our preservation of creation, with an emphasis on the human ecology as the higher good over environmental ecology. Pope Benedict XVI explains:

> If there is a lack of respect for the right to life and to a natural death, if human conception, gestation and birth are made artificial, if human embryos are sacrificed to research, the conscience of society ends up losing the concept of human ecology and, along with it, that of environmental ecology. It is contradictory to insist that future generations respect the natural environment when our educational systems and laws do not help them to respect themselves. The book of nature is one and indivisible: it takes in not only the environment but also life, sexuality, marriage, the family, social relations. . . . Our duties towards the environment are linked to our duties towards the human person, considered in himself and in relation to others. It would be wrong to uphold one set of duties while trampling on the other. Herein lies a grave contradiction in our mentality and practice today: one which demeans the person, disrupts the environment and damages society.[6]

Understanding the dignity of the human person helps us understand the need for the equal dignity of all people, and it is the compelling argument for human rights and freedoms.

The Church has long been the world's leading voice in safeguarding and promoting human rights. One particular document that lists human rights is the encyclical *Centesi-mus Annus* from Pope John Paul II. It lists the most import-ant rights for all human beings on the planet.[7] I take time to list them here because many Catholics cannot name all these rights. The pope has to care for a global Church, and this list helps offer an understanding of what is needed not just in the United States but also around the world.

Those rights of all human persons are

- the right to life, an integral part of which is the right of the child to develop in the mother's womb from the moment of conception;
- the right to live in a united family and in a moral environment conducive to the growth of the child's personality;
- the right to develop one's intelligence and freedom in seeking and knowing the truth;
- the right to share in the work that makes wise use of the earth's material resources and to derive from that work the means to support oneself and one's depen-dents; and
- the right freely to establish a family, to have and to rear children through the responsible exercise of one's sexuality.

Even the briefest review of these rights illustrates how central human dignity is to them all. Pope John Paul II further explains that the overarching right to religious freedom is needed in all countries. "In a certain sense, the source and synthesis of these rights is religious freedom, understood as the right to live in the truth of one's faith and in conformity with one's transcendent dignity as a person."[8]

A CIVILIZATION OF LOVE

The mission of the Church in the world is "helping every human being to discover in God the ultimate meaning of his existence."[9] That existence, inspired by faith, will move a person to change the world, to build a civilization of love. Pope Francis explains that members of the Church ought to be natural change agents in this task. "An authentic faith . . . always involves a deep desire to change the world, to transmit values, to leave this earth somehow better than we found it."[10]

Pope Francis, speaking like a father with concerns for his children who are most in trouble, has likened the Church's activity on earth to a field hospital, tending to those wounded in battle. In his description, we hear an urgent call for dedicated, personal engagement and sacrifice one for another. "I see clearly . . . that the thing the church needs most today is the ability to heal wounds and to warm the hearts of the faithful; it needs nearness, proximity. I see the church as a field hospital after battle. It is useless to ask a seriously injured person if he has high cholesterol and about the level of his blood sugars! You have to heal his wounds. Then we can talk about everything else. Heal the wounds, heal the wounds."[11]

The Church is engaged on a battlefield where love must rule the day if human persons are to do more than survive but also grow and flourish. A civilization of love can only exist where the love permeates all social relationships. True love of neighbor begins with respecting another's dignity.

"The immediate purpose of the Church's social doctrine is to propose the principles and values that can sustain a society worthy of the human person."[12] Notice the order in that last sentence. The goal is not to make human persons worthy of society. It is to make society worthy of human persons. Our human dignity is never, never to be overlooked, undersold, abused, ignored, or hijacked by others in the name of progress, economics, convenience, religion, or politics.

We must always work to safeguard human dignity. The best society for humanity will ultimately be the heavenly one, in union with the fullness of God and one another. But while we are caught up in "the now," awaiting "the not yet," let us work toward building a civilization of love, while maintaining a humble awe of one another.

Again, the saints always get it right. Here's St. Catherine of Siena talking to God about how his love dignifies us: "What made you establish man in so great a dignity? Certainly the incalculable love by which you have looked on your creature in yourself! You are taken with love for her; for by love indeed you created her, by love you have given her a being capable of tasting your eternal Good."[13]

PRAY

Meditate and pray with one or more of these scriptures:

- God creates man and woman in his image; see Genesis 1:26–31.
- God loves orphans, widows, and aliens in foreign lands; see Deuteronomy 10:17–19.
- God made both rich and poor; see Proverbs 22:2.
- Jesus respects the dignity of the Samaritan woman; see John 4:1–42.
- St. James counsels against dishonoring the poor; see James 2:1–8.

LEARN

Read the *Compendium of the Social Doctrine of the Church*, especially chapter 3 on the human person and human rights. Find that in paragraphs 105–159.

The *Compendium* is available in print or on the Vatican website at http://www.vatican.va/roman_curia/pontifical_councils/justpeace/documents/rc_pc_justpeace_doc_20060526_compendio-dott-soc_en.html.

Or discover a new saint whose work promoted human dignity:

> St. Jeanne Jugan
> St. Katharine Drexel
> St. Martin de Porres
> St. Teresa of Calcutta
> St. Vincent de Paul

ENGAGE

Make a donation or become a volunteer with a Catholic aid agency such as the following:

- Catholic Near East Welfare Association (CNEWA) is a papal agency for humanitarian and pastoral support, and it has been a lifeline for the poor throughout the Middle East, Northeast Africa, India, and Eastern Europe for more than ninety years. Go to http://www.cnewa.org.
- Catholic Relief Services carries out the commitment of the bishops of the United States to assist the poor and vulnerable overseas. Go to http://www.crs.org.
- Or find your local St. Vincent de Paul Society in the diocese where you live.

FLYING LESSONS

It's all about the landing—sticking the landing.

I think about that when I see gymnasts fly but most especially when I fly on airplanes. Since 9/11, admittedly, I do a lot of praying before and during the flight. But once we're in the air, I relax and try to enjoy some of the flight, even if I have to do some work. What I love most is the view from the air. I love getting glimpses of God's creation, flying over mountains, plains, lakes, and oceans. I've had wonderful, even prayerful moments as I've soared above fluffy clouds or chased a sunset from coast to coast. Mostly I feel just like a kid up there—very much in awe of flight, especially when I consider how in the world they get that big heavy bird off the ground and then navigate precisely where it needs to go.

I've learned that flying is all about thrust. Without the power of thrust, there is no flight. Thrust is the power to move from one place to another. The way thrust is applied or diminished is key for all phases of flight—the takeoff, the ascent, the level flying, the descent, and the landing. Of the four forces working on that plane—gravity, lift, drag, and thrust—only thrust is generated by the plane's power source. The rest are forces that act on the plane's size and shape and weight as it moves in the air.

Flying is all about the destination. I want to arrive safe and sound, and I want to see loved ones or the happy faces of colleagues on the other side.

Flying is all about who you have with you, too. Some of us are business travelers, and we have our heads down, getting work done. Some of us are family or friends traveling for pleasure.

All of us flyers are pilgrims in a way, making our journey together. Our lives are thrown together by circumstances, often not within our control, for this short voyage.

Months back, I was flying economy class into Atlanta, one of the largest and busiest airports in the United States. There were heavy storms and fog. We had made more than one go-round to prepare to land, and the crew was getting flak from some passengers because there had already been many delays with this flight before takeoff and now there were delays at its end with the weather.

After doing a few donuts in the air, we received clearance to start our final descent. I'm pretty sure the crew in the cockpit was flying on instruments because the mush we were flying through didn't even allow us to see the wingtips from the cabin windows. The pilot warned us via the intercom that things were going to get bumpy on the way down, and he cautioned his crew to buckle up.

The prediction was accurate. There were jerks and shudders and what seemed like one plummeting drop followed by a correction. It was an experience where I felt the magnitude of knowing my life was in the hands of others, and I prayed their skill set and precision were up to the task.

Down, down, down we went.

The cabin got pretty quiet save for the distant whine of the jet engines and a few mothers reassuring antsy children. People who were sleeping were now very much awake—and silent.

I was hoping that as we dropped below the storm cloud cover we'd be able to see better out the window. It didn't happen. A few folks around me made eye contact, looking concerned. I lifted another prayer heavenward and closed my eyes. I tried to pinch my nose and swallow to normalize the screaming pressure in my ears.

Boom!

I was so rattled by the unexpected jolt and bounce on the landing that I wondered if my seat came unhinged. The floor under my feet vibrated with the familiar increasing energy of the reverse thrusters slowing down the jet engines, and I could feel the rush of power that brought us there. Other passengers were just as startled as I was . . . no one had known how close we were to our final destination but those pilots and the air-traffic controllers!

A little bit further down the runway, the flight attendant, clearing her throat over the intercom as if she had lost her voice, let out a sigh of relief. "We're here," she said—an understatement.

Regaining composure, she politely resumed her official arrival greeting for Atlanta. There were more than a few cries, hoots, and nervous laughter from the passengers as the plane slowed to taxi speed.

OUR FLIGHT TO HEAVEN

I often think of that landing—the actual point of arrival shielded from view and the great confidence every passenger and crewmember needed to have in the pilot and copilot that day. It's a lot like our life in the Church. We've all climbed aboard this large and powerful ship in order to reach our destination. We've all got a ticket—Baptism—stamped with the same destination: heaven!

The pilot of the Church is Jesus, and his copilot is the Holy Spirit. We need to trust in them to guide the plane to its final destination. The Pilot and Copilot know how the jet engines work because they are powered by the divine life—the grace of God. The jet engines run on scripture and tradition—that special mixture of jet fuel custom-made for this aircraft.

The individual rows that passengers are seated in are like parishes and dioceses. We don't often get to choose our seating assignment. And even if we did, there is no promise that seat we did select won't be changed. It's often a surprise to discover who is sitting with us or in nearby rows.

Your seat belt is your intellect and your will. It keeps you attached to the plane in flight. You chose to board, and now you are asked to comply with the safety rules for your own safety and that of your fellow passengers.

The mandatory preflight instruction is your Sunday obligation to attend Mass. But remember, going through the motions during that instruction time will not help you in a future emergency, so pay attention and try to learn something new.

The flight attendants are like the priests who serve us nourishing food and drink. They also remind us of all we need to do to enjoy the flight and to arrive at our destination safely. Their words and actions need to be in union with the flight plan and the pilot's directives; otherwise, the flight might be rerouted or late on arrival—or worse.

The folks in the tower offer confidence, warnings, and protections. Our plane takes off and lands with their help and intercessions. These are the saints and angels in heaven.

There's a long history that preceded our arrival at the airport. The ground crew showed up long before we did. Not to mention, the plane's manufacturer prepared for this flight years before the airline ever bought the plane and scheduled our flight. These are like all those who have gone before us in the history of salvation. We cannot fly in this plane without the ones who prepared the way for us to come along.

We carry bags: we go through life with certain attachments to things. But as any frequent flyer will tell you, the less baggage you carry, the sweeter the journey. Those reminders to check your bags are just like reminders to go to confession! Don't be carrying heavy bags on this trip!

Again, the passengers are fellow pilgrims on the journey. Their dignity deserves our respect. We can choose to be kind and helpful and cheerful, or we can be grumpy and resentful of needing to share this particular space with these particular people. We can choose to have a good flight—to obey the rules and cooperate—or we can be selfish and fume.

Or we can rebel and bail. Jumping out and bailing leaves it up to chance and your own skills to try to stick the landing in whatever territory you land in. Or it might feel as if it's all just too much trouble, so we never quite get to the airport and never get on the plane at all. We have the power to choose.

The Church is the perfectly suited conveyance to bring future saints to heaven. Through it, God is determined to give mere mortals the means to live for him. The Church brings us to a place totally different from where we started. It brings us to our "final destination"—heaven.

When the plane finally lands in heaven, even if it has been a bumpy ride to get there, we will be happy when we pass through the gate. For it is our Father who will be running up to meet us at the gate, rejoicing in our coming to live with him forever!

Jesus will step out of the cockpit and switch his captain's hat for a crown, as the Holy Spirit swoops in and—in a flashy yet tasteful way—transforms the airport's arrival area into the most exquisite wedding banquet that heaven has ever seen.

There will be a choir of angels singing the most beautiful music we've ever known. And suddenly we will all be dressed in white.

And we will hear the Beloved One, Jesus, saying to his Father, "This is my Bride, in whom I am well pleased."

THE LIMITS OF ANALOGY AND THE UNLIMITED POWER OF GOD

Okay, so maybe some parts of that flying analogy don't work for you. I was having fun with it. As I said before, all analogies limp—none are perfect.

Yet the truth of the matter is that we put our confidence in so many things of lesser value than the Church, the Mystical Body of Christ.

We step on airplanes all the time and place our trust in a company and a team of people to fly us in the sky—in the *sky*!

We place our money in a bank and leave it there.

We put our identity online.

We vote for the candidate of our choice.

We sign the medical release in hopes of a cure.

We do all these things, and at times all of them have failed us in big, even catastrophic ways. And yet we muster some kind of forgiveness or clemency to invest ourselves all over again in flight, in banking, in online conversations, in politics, in medicine.

When we put our trust in the Church, we do so confidently because we have first put our trust in Christ. When we love the Church, we do so because we want to love what Jesus loves. And we desire the graces that flow from living in communion with Jesus and his Bride.

Yes, of course, there are sinful people in the Church, and they do mess up. Humans sin big. But God's forgiveness is always bigger. Just remember the Cross. There we crucified God. And there we are forgiven. "The Church is not a communion of those 'who have no need of a physician' (Mk 2:17) but a communion of converted sinners who live by the grace of forgiveness and transmit it themselves."[1] That's why staying with the Church means so much to so many—because Jesus Christ is there, standing right beside every earthbound Church member who is a sinner, but a *loved* sinner. We are beggars who know where there is bread. We are wounded who know where there is salve. If you need some, just ask.

Trust in the Church is all about thrust.

The all-in Catholic knows that the thrust of the Church is backed by the full power and providence of the Spirit of God. There is no surer energy. It is unlimited and omnipotent, not weak and misguided. Our misgivings and fears and doubts are no match for the power of God, the Three-in-One Blessed Trinity.

One Fine Day

Jesus went all in out of love for us, to bring us all into his Church where his kingdom "already exists and will be fulfilled at the end of time. The kingdom has come in the person of Christ and grows mysteriously in the hearts of those incorporated into him, until its full . . . manifestation" (*CCC*, 865).

Jesus has paid the price for your ticket. All you have to do is climb aboard and find your seat.

On arrival you will finally know and fully understand the power of the love that brought you there because, on that one fine day and forever, heaven will be your one thing—where the Beloved Bridegroom is never separated from the Bride, where the plan comes together and you will be a beloved child in a perfect family, where divine friendship and divine light will fill every desire and every longing, where love will be for all and in all and all will have enough to infinity and beyond—for you are blessed by your Father, who recognizes you because something of his glory shines on your face.

PRAY

Meditate on Revelation 21:1–7. Write down any themes that are meaningful to you.

LEARN

Pick a book to read next from the resources in the back of this book.

ENGAGE

Choose one of the following:

- Answer the questions from the introduction again.
- Write down one thing from this book that may have moved you forward, if anything, toward a closer relationship with Christ or the Church.
- Pray to the Holy Spirit asking for guidance on what your next step might be.
- Spend ten minutes each day for one month praying with the daily gospel from Mass. And if you can, do that for one year. Find the daily readings at http://www.usccb.org/bible/readings.

ACKNOWLEDGMENTS

Many thanks to Bob Hamma, my friendly editor and fellow cheesecake lover. I wish you joy and peace as you retire after decades of service as Ave Maria Press's Editorial Director. Thank you for making *All In* one of your last titles and for your gracious support for *Blessed, Beautiful, and Bodacious*. Go with God, good man. You will be missed!

Nobody publishes a book alone, so once again it is a privilege to offer my thanks to publisher Tom Grady and especially the editorial, marketing, and creative design teams at Ave Maria Press for your fine work. And hey, you're all just nice to be around!

Looking back, I want to thank the many inspiring and faith-filled adults in my home parish growing up at St. Pius X in Plainview, New York, especially all those who participated in Antioch Weekends and the House of Prayer.

Thank you to the many good priests and people in the parishes where we've lived both in New York and Massachusetts. You prayed with our family and became family along the way. A special shout out to all the Mothers' Morning of Prayer group members near and far! Oh, how the years go by!

More recently, a dose of thanksgiving belongs to my local parish Bible-study members for all your prayers and encouragement.

I couldn't get on the road, speak, or lead retreats without my dedicated intercessory prayer team. Thank you for fortifying my apostolate with your prayers, notes, and unseen sacrifices. You have helped to coax this book out of me!

Thanks, too, to my readership, online and in print, and to my listeners to the *Among Women* podcast. Thank you for subscribing! I'm grateful for our conversations together. A special hello to my friends on Facebook and Twitter!

To my fellow writers and editors, thanks for the collaborations we've had in recent years!

I offer my sincere appreciation to the kind persons who've endorsed this book.

To Maria Morera Johnson, my boon companion, writing buddy, and copy critic, thanks for the friendship and the beach walks.

To my parents, sisters, and dear extended family, thank you for all the solid and silly Catholic stuff along the way. I hope there's something for each of you in these pages.

Heartfelt gratitude to my children and the ever-growing circle of love that our family is becoming! I like having grown children! I am so blessed to be your mom and look forward to happy times ahead!

To my love, Bob—you've been so much a part of my growth as a Christian, and your dedication to Christ and our family is my daily inspiration. Thanks for your encouragement and patience with my writing and my working in fits and starts this past year and for bringing me through my recent hip surgery. I got it repaired so we could drive off into the sunset together. So get the keys to the MG and let's go!

NOTES

INTRODUCTION: WHAT'S DRIVING THIS BOOK?

1. *Catechism of the Catholic Church*, 2nd ed. (Washington, DC: The United States Conference of Catholic Bishops / Libreria Editrice Vaticana, 1997), 36. Future references to the *Catechism* will be made in the text using the abbreviation CCC.

2. John Paul II, Address, "Meeting with the Young People of Malawi," May 5, 1989, 6–7. http://w2.vatican.va/content/john-paul-ii/en/speeches/1989/may/documents/hf_jp-ii_spe_19890505_giovani-malawi.html.

1. THE BELOVED

1. Francis, *Evangelii Gaudium*, 264. http://w2.vatican.va/content/francesco/en/apost_exhortations/documents/papa-francesco_esortazione-ap_20131124_evangelii-gaudium.html.

2. GOD'S LOVE MADE VISIBLE

1. Paul VI, *Lumen Gentium*, 7. http://www.vatican.va/archive/hist_councils/ii_vatican_council/documents/vat-ii_const_19641121_lumen-gentium_en.html.

2. From a homily by Bernard of Clairvaux used in the *Liturgy of the Hours*, Office of Readings, Feast of Our Lady of the Rosary, October 7, vol. 4 (New York: Catholic Book Publishing Corp., 1975) 1471.

3. Gregory of Nyssa, *Oratio Catechetica*, 15, as found in the *Catechism of the Catholic Church*, 457.

4. "Glossary" in *Catechism of the Catholic Church*, s.v. "incarnation."

5. Ibid.

6. Paul VI, *Sacrosanctum Concilium*, 2. http://www. vatican.va/archive/hist_councils/ii_vatican_council/ documentsvat-ii_const_19631204_sacrosanctum-concilium_en.html.

7. Paul VI, *Lumen Gentium*, 8.

8. Ibid.

9. Benedict XVI, quoted in Peter Seewald, "The Pope in His Own Words," *The Telegraph*, November 20, 2010. http://www.telegraph.co.uk/news/newstopics/religion/ the-pope/8148975/The-Pope-in-his-own-words.html.

3. CONFIDENCE IN GOD'S PLAN

1. Francis, "Morning Meditation," April 24, 2013. http://w2.vatican.va/content/francesco/en/cotidie/2013/documents/papa-francesco-cotdie_20130424_ church-mother.html

2. From a sermon by St. Peter Chrysologus (*Sermo* 148). "The Sacrament of Christ's Incarnation" is used in the *Liturgy of the Hours*, Office of Readings, July 30, vol. 3, 1563–64.

3. *Liturgy of the Hours*, Antiphon I, Evening Prayer, January 1, Vol. 1, 477.

4. THE FATHERHOOD OF GOD

1. Find the complete Rite of Baptism here: http:// www.ibreviary.com/m/preghiere.php?tipo=Rito&id=103. Consult your local Roman Catholic Church for complete details on how the Rite of Baptism is performed in your diocese.

2. Patrick Madrid, *Now What? A Guide for New (and Not-So-New) Catholics* (Cincinnati, OH: Servant, 2015), 63.

5. THE MOTHERHOOD OF THE CHURCH

1. Pat Gohn, *Blessed, Beautiful, and Bodacious: Celebrating the Gift of Catholic Womanhood* (Notre Dame, IN: Ave Maria Press, 2013).

2. Christoph Schönborn, *Loving the Church* (San Francisco: Ignatius Press, 1998), 65.

3. John Paul II, *Redemptoris Mater*, 1. http://w2.vatican.va/content/john-paul-ii/en/encyclicals/documents/hf_jp-ii_enc_25031987_redemptoris-mater.html.

4. Pius X, *Ad Diem Illum Laetissimum*, 10, emphasis mine. http://w2.vatican.va/content/pius-x/en/encyclicals/documents/hf_p-x_enc_02021904_ad-diem-illum-laetissimum.html.

5. Benedict XVI, General Audience, January 2, 2008. http://w2.vatican.va/content/benedict-xvi/en/audiences/2008/documents/hf_ben-xvi_aud_20080102.html.

6. Henri de Lubac, S.J., *The Splendor of the Church*, trans. Michael Mason (San Francisco: Ignatius Press, 1999), 322.

7. Henri de Lubac, S.J., *The Motherhood of the Church*, trans. Sergia Englund, O.C.D. (San Francisco: Ignatius Press, 1982), 39.

8. Francis, General Audience, September 3, 2014. http://w2.vatican.va/content/francesco/en/audiences/2014/documents/papa-francesco_20140903_udienza-generale.html.

9. Clement of Alexandria, cited in de Lubac, *Motherhood of the Church*, 74.

10. Origen, cited in de Lubac, *Motherhood of the Church*, 49.

11. Augustine of Hippo, cited in de Lubac, *Motherhood of the Church*, 49–50.

12. Henri Nouwen, S.J., "Forgiving the Church." http://henrinouwen.org/meditation/forgiving-the-church/.

13. Francis, *Lumen Fidei*, 38. http://w2.vatican.va/content/francesco/en/encyclicals/documents/papa-francesco_20130629_enciclica-lumen-fidei.html.

14. Vatican City State, "St. Peter's Square." http://
www.vaticanstate.va/content/vaticanstate/en/monu-
menti/basilica-di-s-pietro/la-piazza.html.

15. John XXVIII, *Mater and Magistra*, 1. http://w2.vat-
ican.va/content/john-xxiii/en/encylclicals/documents/
hf_j-xxxiiienc_15051961_mater.html.

16. de Lubac, *Motherhood of the Church*, 61.

17. Ibid., 72.

18. Ibid., 73.

6. THE DIVINE FRIEND

1. This description for MRI comes from the Mayo
Clinic website: "Magnetic resonance imaging (MRI) is a
technique that uses a magnetic field and radio waves to
create detailed images of the organs and tissues within
your body. Most MRI machines are large, tube-shaped
magnets. When you lie inside an MRI machine, the magnetic field temporarily realigns hydrogen atoms in your
body. Radio waves cause these aligned atoms to produce
very faint signals, which are used to create cross-sec-
tional MRI images—like slices in a loaf of bread. The MRI
machine can also be used to produce 3-D images that may
be viewed from many different angles." http://www.
mayoclinic.org/tests-procedures/mri/basics/definition/
prc-20012903.

2. Benedict XVI, Homily, World Youth Day,
August 21, 2011. http://w2.vatican.va/content/
benedict-xvi/en/homilies/2011/documents/hf_ben-xvi_
hom_20110821_xxvi-gmg-madrid.html

3. Ibid.

4. Francis, cited in Kerri Lenartowick, "To Know
Jesus, We Must Follow Him, Says Pope Francis," *Catholic News Agency*, February 20, 2014. http://www.
catholicnewsagency.com/news-to-know-jesus-we-must-
follow-him-says-pope-francis.

5. Benedict XVI, *Spe Salvi*, 33. http://w2.vatican.va/content/benedict-xvi/en/encyclicals/documents/hf_ben-xvi_enc_20071130_spe-salvi.html

7. THE MYSTICAL BODY OF CHRIST

1. Paul VI, *Lumen Gentium*, 1.

2. "Glossary" in *Catechism of the Catholic Church*, s.v. "purgatory."

3. de Lubac, *Splendor of the Church*, 132.

4. "Glossary" in *Catechism of the Catholic Church*, s.v. "sacrament."

5. Joseph Ratzinger, *Called to Communion: Understanding the Church Today* (San Francisco: Ignatius Press, 1996), 37.

6. Pius XII, *Mystici Corporis Christi*, 83. http://w2.vatican.va/content/pius-xii/en/encyclicals/documents/hf_p-xii_enc_29061943_mystici-corporis-christi.html.

7. See Jn 15:5: "I am the vine, you are the branches. Those who abide in me and I in them bear much fruit, because apart from me you can do nothing."

8. LOVE OF NEIGHBOR

1. Find out more at www.divinemercy.org.

2. Find more about St. Faustina's life and canonization at the Vatican website. http://www.vatican.va/news_services/liturgy/saints/ns_lit_doc_20000430_faustina_en.html.

3. St. Maria Faustina Kowalska, *Diary: Divine Mercy in My Soul* (Stockbridge, MA: Marian Fathers of the Immaculate Conception, 1987), 950.

4. The Chaplet of Divine Mercy is a simple series of prayers that Jesus taught to St. Faustina. When we pray it, we remember that God loves us and his mercy is greater than our sins. When we pray with trust and receive mercy, we can share it with others. To find out more about the Chaplet, go to http://www.thedivinemercy.org/message/devotions/praythechaplet.php.

5. Madeleine Delbrêl, *The Joy of Believing*, English version by Ralph Wright, O.S.B. (Sherbrook, Quebec: Éditions Paulines, 1993), 77.

6. Benedict XVI, *Deus Caritas Est*, 18. http://w2.vatican.va/content/benedict-xvi/en/encyclicals/documents/hf_ben-xvi_enc_20051225_deus-caritas-est.html.

7. From a sermon by Fulgentius of Ruspe, (*Sermo* 3, 1–3, 5–6) used in the *Liturgy of the Hours*, Office of Readings, December 26, vol. 1, 1256–57.

8. Ibid.

9. Ibid.

10. Ibid.

CHAPTER 9

1. Paul VI, *Gaudium et Spes*, 76. http:www.vatican.va/archive/hist_councils/ii_vatican-council/documents/vat-ii-const_19651207_gaudium-et-spec_en.html. See also Pontifical Council for Justice and Peace, *Compendium of the Social Doctrine of the Church* (Washington, DC: The United States Catholic Conference of Bishops/ Libreria Editrice Vaticana, 2005), 21.

2. From a treatise by Robert Bellarmine (*On the Ascent of the Mind to God*) used in the Liturgy of the Hours, Office of Readings, September 17, Vol. 4, 1412.

3. Paul VI, *Gaudium et Spes*, 22.

4. Pontifical Council, *Compendium*, 144.

5. Paul VI, *Gaudium et Spes*, 40.

6. Benedict XVI, *Caritas in Veritate*, 51. http://w2.vatican.va/content/benedict-xvi/en/encyclicals/documents/hf_ben-xvi_enc_20090629_caritas-in-veritate.html.

7. John Paul II, *Centesimus Annus*, 41. http://w2.vatican.va/content/john-paul-ii/en/encyclicals/documents/hf_jp-ii_enc_01051991_centesimus-annus.html.

8. Ibid.

9. Pontifical Council, *Compendium*, 576.

10. Francis, *Evangelli Gaudium*, 183.

11. Francis, cited in Antonio Spadaro, S.J., "A Big Heart Open to God: The Exclusive Interview with Pope Francis," *America*, September 30, 2013. http://america magazine.org/pope-interview.

12. Pontifical Council, *Compendium*, 580.

13. *Catechism of the Catholic Church*, 356.

CONCLUSION

1. Ratzinger, *Called to Communion*, 37.

Resources

Church Teaching

The Bible

A list of translations approved by the United States Conference of Catholic Bishops is found at http://www.usccb.org/bible/approved-translations.

The *New Revised Standard Version, Catholic Edition* (NRSVCE), can be found online at https://www.biblegateway.com/versions/New-Revised-Standard-Version-Catholic-Edition-NRSVCE-Bible.

The *New American Bible, Revised Edition* (NABRE), can be found online at http://www.usccb.org/bible/books-of-the-bible.

The Catechism of the Catholic Church

The *Catechism of the Catholic Church*. 2nd ed. Washington, DC: The United States Conference of Catholic Bishops / Libreria Editrice Vaticana, 1997.

The *Catechism* can also be found online at http://www.vatican.va/archive/ENG0015/_INDEX.HTM or http://www.scborromeo.org/ccc.htm.

The Liturgy of the Hours

The *Liturgy of the Hours*, Vols. I–IV. New York: Catholic Book Publishing Corp., 1975. Page references in the notes refer to this edition.

THE DOCUMENTS OF VATICAN II, ESPECIALLY *LUMEN GENTIUM* AND *GAUDIUM ET SPES*

Available in numerous print editions, and online at http://www.vatican.va/archive/hist_councils/ii_vatican_council/index.htm.

COMPENDIUM OF THE SOCIAL DOCTRINE OF THE CHURCH

Pontifical Council for Justice and Peace. *Compendium of the Social Doctrine of the Church.* Washington, DC: The United States Catholic Conference of Bishops / Libreria Editrice Vaticana, 2005. Also online at http://www.vatican.va/roman_curia/pontifical_councils/justpeace/documents/rc_pc_justpeace_doc_20060526_compendio-dott-soc_en.html.

COMMENTARY ON THE NATURE AND MISSION OF THE CHURCH

de Lubac, S.J., Henri. *The Motherhood of the Church.* Translated by Sergia Englund, O.C.D. San Francisco: Ignatius Press, 1982.

—— *The Splendor of the Church.* Translated by Michael Mason. San Francisco: Ignatius Press, 1999.

Madrid, Patrick. *Why Be Catholic?* Cincinnati, OH: Servant Books, 2015.

Martin, Regis. *What Is the Church: Confessions of a Cradle Catholic.* Steubenville, OH: Emmaus Road Publishing, 2003.

Ratzinger, Joseph. *Called to Communion: Understanding the Church Today.* San Francisco: Ignatius Press, 1996.

Schönborn, Christoph. *Loving the Church.* San Francisco: Ignatius Press, 1998.

GENERAL INTEREST

Catholics Come Home is an apostolate that helps people discover the beautiful faith of the Catholic Church using videos, articles, and books. Visit *www.Catholics ComeHome.org.*

Barron, Robert. *Catholicism.* New York: Image, 2014.

Benedict XVI. *Let's Become Friends of Jesus: Meditations on Prayer.* Frederick, MD: Word Among Us Press, 2013.

Kreeft, Peter. *Catholic Christianity.* San Francisco: Ignatius Press, 2001.

Sheed, Fulton J. *Theology for Beginners.* Kettering, OH: Angelico Press, 2013.

Pat Gohn is a Catholic writer, retreat leader, conference speaker, catechist, and author of the award-winning book *Blessed, Beautiful, and Boducious.*

Host of the *Among Women* podcast, she also is a frequent guest on Catholic radio and television. Her writing has appeared in a number of Catholic publications and blogs, including *Catholic Digest, Catechist, CatholicMom. com, Patheos,* and *Amazing Catechists.* Gohn also has contributed to eight books in recent years, including *Walk in Her Sandals, The Catholic Mom's Prayer Companion,* and *Word by Word.* She is the editor of *Catechist* magazine.

Gohn earned a master's degree in theology and certificates in adult faith leadership, theology of the body, and spiritual direction. She and her husband, Bob, are empty nesters in Massachusetts.

AVE
AVE MARIA PRESS

Founded in 1865, Ave Maria Press,
a ministry of the Congregation of
Holy Cross, is a Catholic publishing
company that serves the spiritual and
formative needs of the Church and its
schools, institutions, and ministers;
Christian individuals and families; and
others seeking spiritual nourishment.

For a complete listing of titles from

Ave Maria Press
Sorin Books
Forest of Peace
Christian Classics

visit www.avemariapress.com

AVE MARIA PRESS
Notre Dame, IN
A Ministry of the United States Province of Holy Cross